Over 150 Easy-to-Use
Gospel Plays for Children

"I want to be Jesus!"

Carol Camp Twork

ave maria press   Notre Dame, IN

I would like to dedicate this book to

my parents, Joyce and Bob,

my husband, Dan,

and my sister, Sandy.

You have always believed in me.

Thank you.

Nihil Obstat:
Reverend James K. Mallett, S.T.L., J.D.
Censor Liborum, Diocese of Nashville
20 October 1998

Imprimatur:
Most Reverend Edward U. Kmiec, D.D., S.T.L.
Bishop of Nashville
23 October 1998

The *Nihil Obstat* and *Imprimatur* are official declarations that a book or pamphlet is considered to be free from doctrinal or moral error. It is not necessarily implied that those who have granted the *Nihil Obstat* and *Imprimatur* agree with the contents, opinions, or statements expressed.

Scripture quotations are paraphrased from the *Contemporary English Version*, copyright © American Bible Society, 1991, 1995.

© 1999 by Ave Maria Press, Inc., P.O. Box 428, Notre Dame, IN 46556

International Standard Book Number: 0-87793-691-9

Cover illustration and text design by: Brian C. Conley

Printed and bound in the United States of America.

Contents

Introduction

How to Use This Book

I Want to Be Jesus! contains plays that trace the words and actions of Jesus through the gospels. The plays are based on the Sunday gospels from each of the liturgical cycles. Children enjoy performing in simple plays, especially in connection with the teachings and actions of Jesus contained in the gospels. These plays can be just read aloud, with no practice, or you may want your students to memorize their lines for some of the more familiar gospels.

These plays are intended to be used each week in religious education classes, either on a Sunday or another day. While the plays are most suited for middle school students, they can also be used with younger and older students. Though there isn't a speaking part for everyone in every play, the rest of the group performs the vital task of being the crowd or audience. Remind the students that Jesus' words and actions always attracted many onlookers. With each play are questions that can be used with the children to facilitate discussion and expand on the meaning of the gospel.

Casting the Play

These plays are not just ordinary plays to perform, but plays taken from the sacred scriptures on the life of Jesus. The students should always be reminded of this. As there may not always be a speaking part for everyone, vary the actors who get those roles from week to week. Try to include all the children in some way. Besides performing the play twice with different casts, divide the longer speaking parts (especially of Jesus) among more than one person. If you have a student who is a hesitant reader, give him or her the shorter Jesus part. It is useful to distinguish the person playing the part of Jesus by having the Jesus actor wear a special robe, hold a shepherd's staff, or even just drape a special cloth around his or her neck. Make sure that everyone has the chance to be Jesus at least once during the course year.

If you have a class of younger children who are unable to read, invite them to watch older students perform the play. The younger children should sit close to the action. Some plays have a character with only one short line that can be assigned to a younger child to perform in the play.

Preparing for the Plays

Make sure to have enough copies of the script for each speaking part. If possible, allow the actors to briefly prepare by rehearsing their parts with one another "off stage."

Performing the Plays

Little or no staging and props are needed to perform these plays. Keep the plays simple. Ask the actors to stand before the audience. It is fine for the actors to perform while reading directly from their scripts.

Uses Beyond Sunday

Though these plays follow the liturgical cycle year for the Sunday gospels, they can also be used in other religious education settings that may or may not be held on Sundays. Use the table of contents to help you locate a gospel by theme. For example, if your class is studying parables, the table of contents will lead you to the various parable plays. Or, if the topic is healing or reconciliation, you might spend a whole class time performing all of the healing plays. The appropriate related gospels can be used to accompany the student's praying of the rosary. For example, the first three glorious mysteries are contained under Easter ABC, Ascension ABC, and Pentecost ABC. The Year C Christ the King gospel is appropriate for the fourth mystery (suggesting that if Jesus is willing to share paradise with a common criminal, wouldn't he offer his mother more?). The Year C Fourth Sunday in Advent reading can be used for the coronation of Mary focusing on Elizabeth's words to Mary, "Blessed are you among women."

Discussion Questions

Two discussion questions are included at the bottom of each play. Ask the questions orally and give each person a chance to share. If the group is large, have the children share their responses with a person next to them. After allowing a brief time for discussion, call on volunteers to share either their own response or the response of their partner with the entire group.

As you become more versed in having the children perform these gospel plays, I'd imagine your experience will be a lot like mine. You will find that the children will enter the meeting space anxious to get a part in the play. Most will say, "I want to be Jesus!"

What could be better than that?

Sunday Gospels

(with Christmas and New Year's Gospels)

Year A

The Time Is Coming

Leader: Jesus tells us to always be ready for his return to earth. We must live a good life so that we can always be with Jesus in heaven.

Jesus: When the Son of Man comes, it will be like what happened with Noah. Before the flood, people were eating and drinking and getting married right up until Noah entered the Ark. They were not concerned until the flood came and the water swept them away. It will be like this when the Son of Man comes:

Farmer: I was working in a field with another man and I turned around and he was gone! It must have been Jesus!

Woman: I was grinding grain with another woman and I turned around and she was gone! She was taken up to heaven!

Jesus: Stay awake! You do not know when your Lord is coming. Remember the lesson of the house owner.

House owner: If I knew that a thief was coming tonight to break into my house, I would stand guard and make sure he could not get in.

Jesus: You must be ready in that same way. The Son of Man is coming at the time you least expect.

How do you prepare for the coming of Christ?

When do you prepare for the coming of Christ?

First Sunday in Advent   Year A   Matthew 24:37-44

A Herald in the Desert

Leader: John the Baptist calls on people to change the way they live. They must prepare for the coming of God by living a good life.

Narrator: When it was the appointed time, John the Baptist appeared, preaching in the wilderness of Judaea.

John the Baptist: Reform your lives. The kingdom of God will soon be here.

Narrator: It was John the Baptist that the prophet Isaiah had spoken about when he said,

Voice of Isaiah: Someone is shouting in the desert, "Prepare the road for the Lord. Make a straight path for him."

First Person (*accepting baptism*)**:** John, I am so sorry for my sins.

Second Person: Me too!

First Sadducee: John wears such funny clothes. They look to be made of scratchy camel's hair. He wears a leather belt around his waist and eats grasshoppers and wild honey too.

First Pharisee: I want to be baptized by John.

Second Pharisee: But he tells us to confess our sins! Why? We are people of Israel and Abraham was our forefather! We are special people.

John the Baptist: I see you Sadducees and Pharisees coming to be baptized. You are like a bunch of snakes. Who told you to run from the wrath of God? You must show that you will live a better life. Don't just say that you belong to the family of Abraham. I tell you that God can turn these stones into children of Abraham. Any tree that is not fruitful will be cut down with an ax and thrown into the fire. I baptize you with water so you will give up your sins. But someone more powerful than I is coming. I am not worthy to carry his sandals. He will baptize you with the Holy Spirit and with fire. He is ready to separate the good grain from the chaff and he will burn the chaff in a fire that will never go out.

Who is it that is coming to baptize with the Holy Spirit and with fire?

What does it mean to separate the grain from the chaff?

Second Sunday in Advent   Years A and B   Matthew 3:1-12/Mark 1:1-8

Jesus Begins His Ministry

Leader: The setting for this gospel reading is the beginning of Jesus' ministry, just after he was baptized in the River Jordan by John the Baptist.

Narrator: While he was in prison, John sent a messenger, one of his disciples, to question Jesus.

Messenger: Jesus, John is in jail. He has asked me to come to you with this question: Are you the one who is to come, or are we to look for someone else?

Jesus: Go and tell John what you have heard and seen: the blind can see, cripples can walk, lepers are cured, the deaf can hear, the dead are raised to life, and the poor hear the good news. God will bless those who do not reject me.

Narrator: The messenger went back to tell John what Jesus had said. Then, Jesus spoke to the crowd.

Jesus: What did you go out in the desert to see?

First Person: A tall grass blowing in the wind.

Second Person: Someone dressed in fine clothes.

Jesus: Remember, those who dress in fine clothes live in royal palaces. What about you? What did you go out in the desert to see?

Third Person: A prophet.

Jesus: Yes, John is a prophet and even more than that. In the scriptures, God says, "I send my messenger ahead of you to prepare your way before you." I tell you that there is no one on this earth who is greater than John the Baptist. But whoever is least in the kingdom of God is greater than John.

Who is the messenger sent to prepare the way for Jesus?

What does Jesus mean when he says that the least in the kingdom of God is greater than John?

Third Sunday in Advent   Year A   Matthew 11:2-11

Joseph's Dream About Jesus

Leader: Over and over the prophets of the Old Testament told people about one who would come and save the people of the world. In this gospel, we hear what one of the prophets had to say about the birth of Jesus.

Narrator: This is how the birth of Jesus Christ came about. Mary and Joseph were engaged to be married.

Mary: Joseph, even though we are not married yet, I am going to have a baby. This will happen through the power of the Holy Spirit.

Narrator: Joseph was a good man and he did not want to embarrass Mary in front of everyone. He was going to quietly call off the wedding. That night, an angel came to Joseph while he was sleeping. The angel said,

Angel: Joseph, son of David, do not fear about taking Mary to be your wife. This child was conceived by the Holy Spirit. She will have a son and you will name him Jesus because he will save people from their sins.

Narrator: This was done to fulfill what the prophet had said,

Voice of Prophet: "The virgin shall be with child and give birth to a son, and they shall call him Emmanuel."

Narrator: The name Emmanuel means "God is with us."

Joseph (*awaking from his sleep*)**:** I will take Mary to be my wife.

Why did the angel give Joseph a message?

What would you have done if you were Joseph?

Fourth Sunday in Advent   Year A   Matthew 1:18-20

The Nativity

Leader: Today a Savior has been born to you. Alleluia! Alleluia!

Narrator: In those days Caesar Augustus published a decree ordering a census of the whole world. This first census took place while Quirinius was governing Syria. Everyone went to register, each to his own town. And so Joseph went from the town of Nazareth to Galilee to Judea, to David's town of Bethlehem because he was of the family of David. He went there with his wife Mary who was with child. While they were there the days of her confinement ended. She gave birth to her first-born and wrapped him in swaddling clothes and laid him in a manger, because there was no room for them in the place where travelers lodged.

Mary and Joseph enter and kneel by a cradle (manger). The room should be darkened and a flashlight placed in the cradle as the only light. The narrator continues.

There were shepherds in the area, living in the fields and keeping night watch by turns over their flock. The angel of the Lord appeared to them, as the glory of the Lord shone around them, and they were very much afraid. The angel said to them,

Angel: You have nothing to fear! I come to proclaim good news to you—tidings of great joy to be shared with everyone. This day in David's city a savior has been born to you, the Messiah and Lord. Let this be a sign to you: in a manger you will find an infant wrapped in swaddling clothes.

The shepherds kneel at the manger. Several angels come on stage.

Narrator: Suddenly there was with the angel a multitude of the heavenly hosts, praising God and saying,

Angels *(together)*: Glory to God in high heaven, peace on earth on whom his favor rests.

---

*Note: This gospel play is taken from the **Lectionary**. Older students are recommended for the reading parts, while younger students can portray Mary, Joseph, the shepherds, and angels. Also, very small children can take the part of stars (holding decorative stars made from cardboard and spray painted gold or silver). This play might be performed to the congregation, but it should be practiced first and the speaking parts should be memorized.*

Christmas Mass at Midnight   Years A, B, and C   Luke 2:1-14

In the Beginning Was the Word

Leader: Today we celebrate the birth of Christ. As the gospel reminds us, Jesus was with God the Father from all time.

Narrator: In the beginning was the Word; the Word was with God and the Word was God. He was with God in the beginning. All things were made with the Word and nothing was made without the Word. Everything that was created received its life from him and his life gave light to everyone. The light shines on in the darkness and the darkness cannot put it out. A man named John was sent to tell everyone about this light.

John the Baptist: I have come to tell you about someone else who is coming. He is the light of the world. I am not the light, I have come to tell you about the light.

Jesus: I am the light of the world. I have been in the world since the beginning, but the world does not know who I am. The people from my own country did not welcome me. Everyone who does accept me is a child of God.

Narrator: The Word became a man and lived in the world with us. We have seen his glory, the glory of the only Son of the Father.

John the Baptist: This is who I have been telling you about. He is greater than I because he was alive before I was born. We have been given many blessings because of Jesus. Moses gave us the law but Jesus Christ showed us kindness and truth that we do not deserve. No one has ever seen God, but we have seen his son and he has shown us what God is like.

Who is the Word?

When did the Word come to be?

Christmas Day   Years A, B, and C   John 1:1-18

Joseph Takes His Family to Egypt

Leader: In this gospel Joseph receives warnings in a dream about people who want to harm the infant Jesus. Joseph and Mary travel great distances to keep Jesus safe.

Narrator: As Mary and Joseph were sleeping, an angel appeared to Joseph in a dream.

Angel: Get up. Take the child and his mother to Egypt. Stay there until I tell you it is safe to leave Egypt. Herod is looking for the child and wants to kill him.

Joseph: Mary! Wake up! We must leave tonight for Egypt.

Narrator: Mary and Joseph began the journey to Egypt. This was to fulfill what the prophet had said,

Voice of Prophet: I will call my son from Egypt.

Narrator: While they were in Egypt, the angel of the Lord spoke to Joseph again in a dream.

Angel: Wake! Take the child and his mother back to Israel. The people who wanted to kill the child are dead.

Narrator: Mary and Joseph readied themselves immediately and returned to Israel. While in Israel Joseph learned that Herod's son had succeeded his father as king. Warned again in a dream, Joseph took Mary and Jesus to a town in Galilee called Nazareth. This was to fulfill what the prophet had said,

Voice of Prophet: He will be called a Nazorean.

What other times did an angel appear to Joseph and Mary with messages?

How would you feel if your family had to move all the time?

Holy Family   Year A   Matthew 2:13-15, 19-23

Mary Remembered These Things

Leader: New Year's Day is a holy day dedicated to Mary, the Mother of God. The gospel reminds us that Mary treasured the events of Jesus' birth in her heart. After receiving a message by the angels, some shepherds visited the place where Jesus was born.

First Shepherd: We must go to Bethlehem and see what the angels were talking about.

Second Shepherd: The angels said we would find the baby in a manger.

Narrator: The shepherds then set off for Bethlehem and found the place where Jesus, Mary, and Joseph were staying.

Third Shepherd: We were told to come and find you.

Fourth Shepherd: The angels said this baby born tonight is the Savior.

Mary: I will remember what you have told me.

First Shepherd *(leaving with the others)***:** We must go back to tend our sheep.

Second Shepherd: Everything is just as the angels told us it would be.

Third Shepherd: Praise God in heaven! He has answered our prayers tonight!

Narrator: Eight days after this event, Joseph said to Mary,

Joseph: It is time to take the baby to the Temple and present him to the Lord. What name shall we give him?

Mary: His name is Jesus. The angel who visited me told me that Jesus should be his name.

How do you think the shepherds felt to see angels in the field, telling them about the birth of the Savior?

How do you think Mary felt when the shepherds visited her baby?

Solemnity of Mary,   Year A   Luke 2:16-21
the Mother of God

The Visit of the Three Wise Men

Leader: An evil king, Herod, was not pleased with the birth of Jesus. He sent three astrologers—or wise men—to seek out the baby so that he could have Jesus put to death. The three wise men traveled a very long way to find him, and their hearts were changed.

First Wise Man: Where is the newborn king of the Jews?

Second Wise Man: We saw his star when it came up in the sky.

Third Wise Man: We must go and honor him.

King Herod *(to himself)*: A newborn king of the Jews? I do not like the sound of that. Could this be the one the Jewish prophet spoke of?

Voice of Prophet: Bethlehem, in the land of Judea, you are very important among the towns of Judea. From your town will come a leader, who will be like a shepherd for my people Israel.

King Herod: I want you to go and find out about this child. When you have found him, come back and report to me. I want to go and honor him too.

First Wise Man: We will follow the star and find the child.

Second Wise Man *(pointing)*: Look, the star is right over that place.

Third Wise Man *(bowing)*: There is the child, with his mother.

First Wise Man: We have come very far to find you. I brought you the gift of gold.

Second Wise Man: We followed your star here. I brought you the gift of frankincense.

Third Wise Man: We believe that this is the child the prophets have told us about. I brought you the gift of myrrh.

Narrator: Later in a dream a messenger informed the wise men,

Messenger: You must not return to Herod, or let him know what you have found out about this child and his family. When you return to your own country, you must go back another way.

Why did Herod really want to find the infant Jesus?

Why do you think the wise men changed their hearts about the baby?

Epiphany   Years A, B, and C   Matthew 2:1-12

The Baptism of the Lord

Preparation: Place a blue streamer or blue piece of yarn on the floor to signify the river. Have the audience stand on both sides of the "river." The actors—John and Jesus—stand in the river.

Leader: Today's gospel tells of the baptism of Jesus by John the Baptist. When this occurred, all three persons of the Holy Trinity—Father, Son, and Holy Spirit—were present.

John the Baptist *(entering the river)*: Someone more important than I is coming soon. I am not worthy to stoop and loosen the straps of his sandals.

Jesus *(kneeling before John)*: **Will you baptize me?**

John the Baptist: I baptize you with water. You have come to baptize with the Holy Spirit.

Onlooker: Look up there! The sky is opening. A spirit, like a dove, is descending on that man, Jesus.

Voice of God *(standing behind Jesus with hands upraised in blessing)*: This is my beloved Son, who has made me very happy.

Why do you think Jesus wanted to be baptized?

What did the dove represent?

First Sunday in Ordinary Time   Years A, B, and C   Matthew 3:13-17
                                                                  Mark 1:6b-11
                                                                  Luke 3:15-16, 21-22

Jesus Spends Forty Days in the Desert

Leader: Lent is a time to walk with Christ. We reconcile ourselves with one another and with God. In the gospel today, we learn how the devil tried to tempt Jesus to sin and how Jesus answered the devil.

Narrator: After Jesus was baptized in the Jordan River, the Holy Spirit led him into the desert. There, Jesus was tested by the devil for forty days. During this time, Jesus had nothing to eat. After the forty days he was hungry. The devil spoke to him,

Devil: If you are the Son of God, turn that stone into bread so that you can eat.

Jesus: Scripture says, "No one needs only food to eat."

Narrator: The devil took Jesus up to a high place.

Devil: If you are God's Son, jump off this rooftop. Because scripture says, "God will make his angels to take care of you. They will catch you in their arms, and you will not even stumble on a stone." So, go ahead and jump, because the angels will take care of you.

Jesus: Scripture also says, "Worship and serve only God." And, "Do not test God."

Narrator: Then the devil left and the angels came to be with Jesus. Jesus traveled to Galilee and told the people,

Jesus: The time has come! Believe in the Good News!

How have you been tempted?

What can you do to prove you love God?

First Sunday of Lent   Years A, B, and C   Matthew 4:1-11
                                                                            Mark 1:12-15
                                                                            Luke 4:1-13

The Transfiguration of Jesus

Leader: In today's gospel Jesus takes his most beloved disciples with him to a mountain to pray. They see something no one else can see, a vision that includes Elijah and Moses, two prophets who lived long before. God's voice corrects their understanding. Jesus tells them not to tell what they saw to anyone.

Jesus: Come with me to the mountaintop to pray.

Narrator: Peter, John, and James went with Jesus as he requested. They noticed something and began to share what they saw.

Peter: Jesus! What has happened to your clothes?

John (*covering his eyes*): They are so white and dazzling they hurt my eyes!

James: I see Elijah and Moses. How can that be?

Peter: Teacher, we are so glad to be here with you. Let us build three shelters: one for you, one for Moses, and one for Elijah.

John (*pointing to the sky as the others look up*): Look at that cloud!

Narrator: God's voice is heard.

Voice of God: This is my Son. I love him. Listen to what he says.

James: Where did Moses go?

Peter: Where did Elijah go?

Jesus: It is time to travel back down the mountain. Do not tell anyone what you saw here today until the Son of Man has been raised up from the dead.

John: Raised up from the dead? What does that mean?

James: Who's going to be raised up from the dead?

Why did Jesus take his friends to the mountaintop?

What does God tell us to do?

Second Sunday of Lent	Years A, B, and C	Matthew 17:1-9
		Mark 9:2-9
		Luke 9:28b-36

The Woman at the Well

Leader: In Jesus' time, the people from Samaria had nothing to do with the Jews, and the Jews had nothing to do with the Samaritans.

Narrator: Jesus traveled through the land of Samaria to a town called Sheckem. The town was near the spot of Jacob's well. Jesus was tired from his long trip and sat down at the well. His disciples had gone into town for food. A woman came from Samaria to get water from the well. Jesus said to her,

Jesus: Please give me a drink of water.

Woman: You are a Jew. How can you ask a Samaritan woman for a drink? Jews and Samaritans usually don't have anything to do with one another.

Jesus: If only you knew what God wants to give you and who is asking you for a drink. You would have asked me for water instead and I would have given you living water.

Woman: You don't even have a bucket and this well is very deep. How do you expect to get this water that gives life? This well was dug by our ancestor Jacob, and his family and animals drank from it. Are you better than he is?

Jesus: Whoever drinks this water will be thirsty again. Whoever drinks the water I give will never be thirsty again. The water I give is like a fountain that gives everlasting life.

Woman: I would like a drink of that water. Then I wouldn't have to keep coming to this well to get water every day.

Jesus: Bring your husband here.

Woman: I don't have a husband.

Jesus: You are right about that. You have been married five times and the man you are living with now is not your husband.

Woman: Sir, I know now that you are a prophet. But my family has always worshipped on this mountain. You Jews say that Jerusalem is the only place to worship God.

Jesus: Believe me, soon you will not worship God on this mountain or in Jerusalem. You people from Samaria don't really know the God you worship. We Jews do know the God we worship, and God will use us to save the world. But even now, the Spirit is leading all true worshippers to God. This pleases God. God is the Spirit, and those who worship him must be led by the Spirit to worship him in truth.

Woman: I know that the Messiah is coming. He will tell us the truth.

Jesus: I am that one, and I am telling you the truth now.

Narrator: Meanwhile, the disciples returned.

First Disciple: Jesus, we are here.

Second Disciple: We have food for our supper. Come with us.

Narrator: The disciples were surprised to see Jesus speaking to the Samaritan woman, but they did not ask him about her. The woman left her water jar and went to tell the people about Jesus.

Woman (*gathering crowd off stage*)**:** Come and see this man! He knows everything about me. He might be the Messiah.

Narrator: The people from the town went out to see Jesus. Meanwhile, the disciples were trying to get Jesus to eat some food.

Third Disciple: Teacher, please eat some supper.

Jesus: I have food to eat that you do not know about.

Fourth Disciple: Did someone else bring him some food to eat?

Jesus: Pleasing God is my food. He sent me and I must finish the work he sent me to do. Don't you look forward to the harvest? The time of harvest is now. This harvest is of eternal life. The one who plants and the one who harvests are celebrating together. There is a saying that is true,

Voice of Saying: One person plants, another person harvests.

Jesus: I am sending you to bring in the harvest from fields where you did not plant the seeds. Other people worked to plant the seeds, but you get to harvest.

First Samaritan (*arriving*)**:** I believe that this man, Jesus, is the Messiah.

Second Samaritan: Stay with us, Jesus. Stay in Samaria.

Narrator: So Jesus stayed in Samaria for two days.

Third Samaritan: Jesus has taught us so much while he is here. I believe now because of what I have heard myself. He really is the Savior of the World.

What is the living water that Jesus talked about?

Name the sacrament that uses water.

Third Sunday of Lent   Year A   John 4:5-42

27

The Man Born Blind

Leader: Today's gospel addresses a question that may have been asked as: "What is sin?"

Narrator: Jesus and his disciples passed a man who had been blind since birth. One of the disciples asked Jesus,

Disciple: Teacher, is he blind because his parents sinned or because he sinned?

Jesus: It was not the sin of anyone that caused this man to be blind. But because he is blind, you will see a miracle from God. *(Jesus spits on the ground and makes mud with his saliva. He places mud on the blind man's eyes. Then he speaks directly to the man.)* **Go and wash in the Siloam pool.**

Narrator: The word Siloam means "one who has been sent." The man went to the pool as Jesus asked him. After washing, the man began to shout out,

Blind man: I can see! I can see!

First Neighbor: Isn't he the blind man who used to sit and beg?

Second Neighbor: No, that's not him, but it looks like him.

Blind Man: I was blind but now I can see. I am the man you are talking about.

Third Neighbor: How were you cured?

Blind Man: The man called Jesus made mud and smeared it on my eyes. Then he told me to wash in the pool of Siloam and when I did, I could see.

Fourth Neighbor: Where is Jesus now?

Blind Man: I don't know.

First Neighbor *(leading everyone to see the Pharisees)*: Come with us to the Pharisees. They need to know that you were cured on the Sabbath.

Narrator: Now the Pharisees questioned the man in a similar way.

First Pharisee: How were you cured?

Blind Man: Jesus put mud on my eyes and when I washed it off, I could see.

Second Pharisee: Jesus did work on the Sabbath. That is a sin. Besides, how could a sinner perform a miracle? Blind man, what do you think about this man, Jesus?

Blind Man: He must be a prophet.

First Pharisee: I don't believe this man was born blind. Send for his parents and ask them. They will know.

Narrator: The blind man's parents were brought to the Pharisees.

Second Pharisee: Is this man your son? Was he born blind?

Blind Man's Father: This is our son and he was blind when he was born. We don't know why he can see now or who cured him.

Blind Man's Mother: Why don't you ask him? He is old enough to speak for himself.

Narrator: The blind man's parents were afraid of the Pharisees. They knew that the Pharisees had decided that anyone who believed that Jesus was the Messiah would be thrown out of the synagogue.

First Pharisee: We are here to give God glory. Tell us that Jesus is a sinner.

Blind Man: I do not know if he is a sinner. I know that I was blind and now I can see.

Second Pharisee: What did he do to you? How did he cure you?

Blind Man: I told you before but you don't want to listen and believe. Why do you want me to tell you again? Do you want to become his disciples?

First Pharisee: You are the one who is his disciple. We are followers of Moses. We know that God spoke to Moses, but we are not sure about Jesus.

Blind Man: Isn't it strange that he healed my eyes but you don't know anything about him? We know that God listens to those who believe in him and love him. He doesn't listen to sinners. No one has ever healed a man who was blind from birth. Jesus could not do such a thing unless he came from God.

First Pharisee: You are a sinner and have been a sinner since you were born. You cannot teach us anything about God. Leave and never come back!

Narrator: The Pharisees threw the man out of the synagogue. Jesus found out where he was and spoke to him.

Jesus: Do you believe in the Son of Man?

Blind Man: I will believe in him if you will show me where he is.

Jesus: You are talking to him now.

Blind Man (*bowing down*)**:** I do believe in you, Lord.

Jesus: I have come to judge this world. I have come to make the people who are blind see, and make the people who can see blind.

Second Pharisee: Are you saying we are blind?

Jesus: You would have no sin if you were blind. But you say you can see. This means you are a sinner.

What reason did Jesus give for the man being blind?

What does Jesus mean when he says he "came to make the people who are blind see, and the people who can see blind"?

Fourth Sunday of Lent   Year A   John 9:1-41

The Raising of Lazarus

Leader: In the raising of Lazarus, Jesus tells us, "I am the resurrection and the life."

Narrator: Jesus' friend Lazarus was very sick. He and his sisters Mary and Martha lived in the village of Bethany. His sisters were taking care of him. Mary was the one who used perfume to wash Jesus' feet and her hair to dry them. After a messenger told Jesus that Lazarus was sick, Jesus said,

Jesus: Lazarus is sick but he will not die. This will bring glory to God and his Son.

Narrator: Even though Jesus loved Lazarus and his sisters, he stayed where he was for two more days before going to them. One of his disciples questioned him,

First Disciple: Teacher, why do you want to go to Bethany? They tried to stone you there the last time.

Jesus: There are twelve hours of sunlight. If we walk in the daytime we will not stumble. But if we walk at night, we will stumble in the dark. I have to go back because my friend Lazarus has fallen asleep and I must wake him.

Second Disciple: If he is asleep, he will get better.

Jesus: I mean that Lazarus is dead. For your sakes I'm glad I wasn't there so that now you will believe. Let us go to him.

Thomas: Oh, for heaven's sake. Let's go and die with Jesus.

Narrator: Jesus and his disciples set out to Bethany. When they arrived, they found out that Lazarus had been in his tomb for four days. Martha came out to meet Jesus.

Martha: Jesus, if you had been here Lazarus would not have died. But I am sure that if you ask God, he will give you whatever you want.

Jesus: Your brother will live.

Martha: I know that he will rise on the last day, when all the dead will rise.

Jesus: I am the resurrection and the life. Whoever believes in me, even if he dies, will come to life, and whoever is alive and believes in me will never die. Do you believe this, Martha?

Martha: Yes, Lord, I believe that you are the Messiah, the Son of God who is to come into the world.

Narrator: Then Martha went and found Mary. Mary and her many visitors went out to where Jesus was. Mary, crying, said to Jesus,

Mary: Lord, if you had been here, my brother would not have died.

Narrator: Jesus was upset to see Mary cry, and began to cry himself.

Jesus *(emotionally)*: Where did you bury him?

First Neighbor: Come and see.

Second Neighbor: See how Jesus loved Lazarus.

Third Neighbor: He cured the blind so they could see. Why didn't he keep Lazarus from dying?

Narrator: By this time Jesus had arrived at the tomb.

Jesus: Roll away the stone from that tomb.

Narrator: After the neighbors rolled the stone away, Jesus prayed.

Jesus: Thank you, Father, for hearing me. I know that you always hear me, but I am praying this out loud so these people can hear me and believe that you sent me. Lazarus! Come out!

Narrator: Lazarus came out of the tomb. He was wrapped in strips of cloth from his burial.

Jesus: Untie him and let him free.

Narrator: Many of the people there saw what Jesus had done, and believed in him.

Why did Jesus wait so long before he went to Lazarus?

Why did Jesus pray out loud?

Fifth Sunday of Lent   Year A   John 11:1-45

Entering Jerusalem

Leader: Jesus knew what would happen when he went to Jerusalem. In today's gospel, Jesus is greeted eagerly by the crowds, though in a few days many in the same crowd would deny him shouting, "Crucify him, crucify him."

Narrator: Jesus and his disciples entered the walled city of Jerusalem. Jesus said to two of his disciples,

Jesus: Go ahead of us to the next village. There will be a young donkey there who has never been ridden. Untie the donkey and bring it here. If anyone asks why you are doing that, tell them, "The Lord needs it."

Narrator: The two disciples went ahead of the others and found the donkey, just as Jesus said. They untied it and took it to Jesus.

First Disciple: Here, Jesus, get on the donkey. There's a crowd of people lining the entranceway into Jerusalem.

Narrator: Jesus rode on the donkey while the disciples followed close by on the parade route.

Second Disciple: Look at all the people who have come to greet Jesus!

First Onlooker: Hosanna! Blessed is the one who comes in the name of the Lord!

Second Onlooker: Hosanna! Praise God in heaven!

Third Onlooker: Hosanna! Blessed is the Son of David!

Narrator: A Pharisee standing nearby was disgusted at what was taking place.

Pharisee: Jesus! Tell the crowd to be quiet.

Jesus: Even if they were to be quiet, the rocks and stones would sing out!

Why did Jesus want to go to Jerusalem if he knew what would happen to him?

Why do you think the attitude of the people changed between this day and Good Friday?

Passion (Palm) Sunday   Years A, B, and C   Matthew 21:1-11
                                                                    Mark 11:1-10
                                                                    Luke 19:29-40

Jesus Is Risen!

Leader: Happy Easter! The first disciples did not understand what we do. They thought Jesus was dead and buried in a tomb. We know that Jesus is risen! Alleluia!

Narrator: Early in the morning on the third day after Jesus died, Mary Magdalene went to the tomb. She had oils to anoint the body and prepare it to be buried.

Mary Magdalene: Someone has removed the stone! I need to tell Peter.

Narrator: Mary Magdalene hurried to find Peter and the other disciples.

Mary Magdalene: Quick! Come and see! Someone has moved the stone. The Lord has been taken away from his tomb and we don't know where they have taken him.

Peter: Come with me! Let's go and see.

Narrator: Peter and John, the disciple that Jesus loved, ran to the tomb. Peter was the slower runner. When he finally got there he said,

Peter: Look! Jesus is not here, but there are pieces of cloth that wrapped his body. There is the cloth that covered his face.

John: I have seen this with my own eyes and I believe that Jesus is risen.

How do you think Mary Magdalene felt when she saw the empty tomb?

Why do you think the disciples believed that Jesus is risen from the dead?

Easter Sunday   Years A, B, and C   John 20:1-9

Doubting Thomas

Leader: After Jesus was crucified, his disciples were afraid. They hid in a locked room. They were afraid the soldiers would come for them too.

First Disciple: Everyone lock the door when you enter this room. The soldiers are trying to find us.

Second Disciple: I am afraid we'll be killed like Jesus was.

Narrator: Jesus suddenly appeared and stood among them.

Jesus: Peace be with you.

Third Disciple: Jesus! It is you! The marks are on your hands and side.

Fourth Disciple: We are so happy to have you here.

Narrator: Jesus breathed on them and said again,

Jesus: Peace be with you. I am sending you as my Father sent me. Receive the Holy Spirit. If you forgive a person's sins, they are forgiven in heaven. But if you don't forgive a person's sins, they will be held bound to those sins.

Narrator: Jesus left the room. Then, shortly afterward the apostle Thomas returned. He had been away.

First Disciple: Thomas, you missed Jesus! He was just here. We saw him.

Thomas: I don't believe it. And I won't ever believe it unless I can probe the nail marks in his hands and put my hand in his side.

Narrator: A week passed. Once again the disciples were all in the locked room. This time Thomas was with them.

Jesus: Peace be with you. Thomas, come here! Take your fingers and probe the nail marks in my hand. Put your hand into my side. I want you to believe!

Thomas: My Lord and my God.

Jesus: You believe because you saw me yourself. Blessed are those who believe without seeing me.

Why were Jesus' disciples afraid?

Who is Jesus talking about? Who believes in him without seeing him?

Second Sunday of Easter   Years A, B, and C   John 20:19-31

The Road to Emmaus

Leader: Today's gospel describes an event that happened shortly after Jesus' resurrection. See if you can recognize Jesus in the story.

Narrator: Two of Jesus' disciples were walking to the village of Emmaus, which is about seven miles from Jerusalem. They did not yet understand all that was going on concerning Jesus.

First Disciple: I can't believe what has happened these past few days.

Second Disciple: Last week Jesus came into Jerusalem on a donkey and all of Jerusalem cheered for him.

First Disciple: Then just a few days later he was crucified and we buried him. Now the tomb is empty. He is not there.

Narrator: A man meets the disciples and starts to walk with them.

Jesus: Why do you look so sad? Why are you so gloomy?

Second Disciple: Are you the only one from Jerusalem who has not heard what has happened?

Jesus: What do you mean?

First Disciple: Haven't you heard what has happened to Jesus from Nazareth? He showed that he was a prophet by what he said and did. Then the chief priests had him arrested and he was sentenced to die on a cross. We were sure that he was the one who was sent to free Israel, but it has already been three days since he died.

Second Disciple: Some of the women with us went to the tomb this morning and found that Jesus' body was not there. They told us that they saw angels who said that Jesus was alive. So some of our friends went there. They didn't find Jesus either. Now we're not sure what happened.

Jesus: Why can't you understand? Don't you remember what Moses and the prophets said? You must have known the Messiah would have to suffer before he was glorified. Let me explain it to you.

Narrator: As they all walked together to Emmaus, Jesus explained the scriptures to them.

First Disciple: Here we are. It is almost dark. Stay with us tonight.

Jesus: All right.

Narrator: Jesus and the two disciples entered the house and sat down for supper.

Jesus: Thank you Lord for this bread we are about to eat.

Narrator: As Jesus broke the bread and said the blessing the disciples recognized him.

Second Disciple: It is the Lord, Jesus.

Narrator: When they said this, Jesus vanished from their sight.

First Disciple: I should have known. When we were walking with him and he explained the scriptures to us, I could tell it was Jesus in my heart.

Second Disciple: We must go back to Jerusalem and tell the others.

Narrator: The disciples traveled back to Jerusalem and spoke with other disciples.

First Disciple: Let us tell you what has happened to us. You will never believe it!

Third Disciple: Jesus is risen! It is true! Simon Peter saw him.

Second Disciple: We saw him, too, on our walk to Emmaus. He walked with us and explained the scriptures to us, but we didn't recognize him until he blessed and broke the bread for us.

Why didn't the two disciples recognize Jesus on their walk to Emmaus?

What do we believe about Jesus when bread is broken and the cup is blessed at Eucharist?

Third Sunday of Easter · Year A · Luke 24:13-35

Jesus, the Sheepgate

Leader: Jesus often referred to himself as the Good Shepherd, someone who watches over the sheep and keeps them from harm. In today's gospel Jesus also describes himself as the gate that all the sheep must go through.

Jesus: Only a thief would climb over a fence to get to the sheep pen instead of going through the gate. The shepherd enters through the gate. The sheep know their shepherd's voice and they come to him when he calls their name. When he has called them all out of the pen, he walks in front of them and they follow him because they know his voice. The sheep will not follow a stranger. They will run away from a stranger.

First Disciple: Jesus, we don't understand what you are trying to tell us.

Jesus: I am the gate for the sheep to pass through. A thief only comes to steal or kill or destroy. I have come so that everyone would have life and have it to the full. The people who came before me were thieves and the sheep did not listen to them. I am the gate. Everyone who enters through me will be saved. They will enter through me and they will find pasture.

How is Jesus like the gate of a sheep pen?

Why is the gate important?

Fourth Sunday of Easter   Year A   John 10:1-10

I Am the Way, the Truth, and the Life

Leader: Jesus is the way, the truth, and the life. We can only know God the Father when we know Jesus.

Jesus: Don't worry. Have faith in the Father and in me. There is room for many in my Father's house. That is why I said I will go and get a room ready for you. Then I will come back and take you there so we can be together. You know the way already.

Thomas: Lord, we don't know where you are going. How can we know the way?

Jesus: I am the way and the truth and the life. Without me you cannot go to the Father. If you knew me, you would know the Father. But now you do know the Father and you have seen him.

Philip: Lord, show us the Father and that will be all that we need.

Jesus: You have been with me all this time. Don't you know who I am? When you see me, you see the Father. Why do you ask me to show the Father to you? Don't you know that I am part of the Father and he is part of me? We are one. What I say doesn't come from me, it comes from the Father. If you have faith in me, you will do what I have been doing. You will do even greater things than I, because I am going back to the Father.

How do we know God the Father?

How do we know what Jesus wants us to do?

Fifth Sunday of Easter   Year A   John 14:1-12

I Will Not Leave You Orphans

Leader: In today's gospel, Jesus tells us how we are to show love for him.

Jesus: If you love me, you will obey my commandments. I will ask the Father to send the Holy Spirit to you. The Spirit will help you and show you the truth. The Spirit will stay with you always. The world will not see the Spirit or know the Spirit and so the world will not believe in the Spirit. But you will know the Spirit because the Spirit will stay with you and will live in you.

First Disciple: Why will we need this Spirit when we have you?

Second Disciple: Are you leaving us?

Jesus: I will not leave you like orphans. I will come back for you. But soon, the world will not be able to see me, but you will see me. You will live because I live. You will know that I am part of the Father. You will be part of me and I will be part of you. If you love me, you will do what I have said and my Father will love you. I will love you too and you will know me.

What should we do if we love Jesus?

Who did Jesus promise to send to his disciples when he returned to the Father?

Sixth Sunday of Easter   Year A   John 14:15-21

The Father and I Are One

Leader: The setting for today's gospel is the Last Supper, immediately before Jesus was betrayed. Jesus offers this prayer to the Father, knowing that his arrest and crucifixion are near.

Jesus: Father, the time has come. Give glory to your Son so he may give glory to you. You gave him power over everyone so he would give eternal life to all those you have trusted him with.

First Disciple: What is eternal life?

Jesus: Eternal life is to know the only you, my Father, and the One you have sent. I have done everything on earth you sent me to do, Father, so that I could give glory to you. Now give me back the glory I had with you before the world was created.

Second Disciple: Now I understand that Jesus was with God before the world was created.

Jesus: I have followers that you, Father, have given me on this earth, and I have shown them what you are like. They were followers of yours but you gave them to me. They still obey your commandments. They know everything I have comes from you. I told my disciples what you told me and they believe it and have faith.

Third Disciple: Yes, we do believe.

Jesus: Father, they know that I came from you and that you sent me. I pray for my followers because they are really your followers. Everything I have is yours and everything that you have is mine. These disciples will bring glory to me. Father, I am not part of this world anymore. I am coming to you. My followers are still a part of this world. I pray that you will keep them safe, by the power of my name. They will be part of one another, just as you and I are part of one another.

What is eternal life?

How long has Jesus been with God the Father?

Seventh Sunday of Easter   Year A   John 17:1-11a

Come, Holy Spirit

Leader: Pentecost is the day fifty days from Easter when the Church first received the Holy Spirit. The Holy Spirit gave the disciples courage to preach the good news of Jesus to the world.

Narrator: On a Sunday evening the doors were closed in the room where the disciples were hiding out of fear of Jesus' enemies. Suddenly Jesus came and stood among them.

Jesus: Peace be with you.

Narrator: Jesus showed his hands and side to the disciples. He breathed on them and said again,

Jesus: Peace be with you. The Father sent me into this world and now I send you to tell everyone what you know. Receive the Holy Spirit. If you forgive anyone's sins they will be forgiven in heaven. If you do not forgive them on earth, they will not be forgiven in heaven.

Why were the disciples hiding and afraid?

What do Jesus' words tell you about the importance of the sacrament of reconciliation?

Pentecost Sunday   Years A, B, and C   John 20:19-23

Holy Trinity

Leader: This gospel is read on Trinity Sunday to tell how God sent his Son to save the world through him.

Narrator: Jesus spoke to Nicodemus, a Jewish leader. Nicodemus had told Jesus that he knew Jesus was sent by God because of all the miracles Jesus had performed. Nicodemus still had many questions about how to enter the kingdom of heaven.

Nicodemus: What will happen to those who believe in you?

Jesus: Everyone who believes in the Son of Man will have eternal life. God loved this world so much that he sent us his Son. Everyone who believes in him will never really die.

Nicodemus: Why did God send his Son to earth?

Jesus: God sent his Son to save people, not to condemn them. No one who has faith in God's Son will be doomed, but everyone who doesn't believe in God's Son is already cursed.

What will happen to those who believe in Jesus?

Why did God send his Son to earth?

Sunday After Pentecost   Year A   John 3:16-18

Corpus Christi

Leader: Jesus tells us, "My flesh is real food and my blood is real drink." *Corpus Christi* is the Latin term for the body and blood of Christ.

Narrator: Jesus told the crowds,

Jesus: I am the living bread from heaven. Everyone who eats this bread will have eternal life. My body is the bread I give to the people of the world so that they may live.

First Person: What does he mean by that?

Second Person: How can he give us his body as bread?

Third Person: How can he give us his body to eat?

Jesus: You will not live unless you eat my body and drink my blood. If you eat my body and drink my blood, you will have everlasting life and I will raise you to life on the last day. My body is real food and my blood is real drink. If you eat my body and drink my blood, you are part of me and I am part of you. I was sent by the Father and I have life because of him. Now, everyone who eats my body will have life because of me. This bread from heaven is not what your ancestors ate. They died, but if you eat this bread from heaven, you will live.

When do we eat the body and drink the blood of Christ?

What does Jesus say happens when we eat his body and drink his blood?

Sunday After Trinity Sunday   Year A   John 6:51-58

Here Is the Lamb of God

Leader: After John the Baptist baptized Jesus in the Jordan River, John tells his own followers that Jesus is the one they have been waiting for. A voice from heaven confirms John's words.

Narrator: The day after he was baptized Jesus approached John.

John the Baptist: Look! Here is the Lamb of God who takes away the sins of the world. This is who I was talking about when I said, "Someone who is greater than me is coming. He was alive before I was born." I didn't know who he was but I was sent ahead of him to baptize him with water so that all the people in Israel would see him. I saw the Spirit like a dove come down from heaven and land on him. I didn't know who he was before that. But the one who sent me to baptize with water also told me,

Voice from Heaven: When you see the Spirit come down from heaven like a dove and rest on someone, that is the person who is sent to baptize with the Holy Spirit.

John the Baptist: I have seen this and I have told you about it. He is the Son of God.

What does John mean when he says of Jesus, "He was alive before I was born"?

How is the Holy Trinity present in this reading?

Second Sunday in Ordinary Time   Year A   John 1:29-34

Jesus Chooses His Disciples

Leader: This gospel reading tells the occasion of Jesus' call of his disciples. You will find out how they responded when Jesus said, "Come with me."

Narrator: After Jesus learned that John the Baptist had been arrested he left Nazareth and went to Capernaum to fulfill the words of the prophet Isaiah.

Voice of Prophet: Listen, people of all nations. Your people live in darkness but they will see a great light and the light will shine on them.

Jesus: The time has come: God's kingdom will soon be here. Turn back to God and believe in the good news.

Narrator: Jesus walked along the lake and spotted some fisherman. He spoke first to Andrew and his brother Simon.

Jesus: Come with me and I will make you fishers of people.

Andrew *(to Simon)*: I want to follow him.

Peter: Let's drop everything and go.

Narrator: Both men left their fishing nets to go with Jesus. Jesus then walked on the shore near where John and James were fishing. Their father Zebedee was also with them.

John: Father, James and I have finished mending the nets. We are going to take the boat out farther and fish some more before it gets dark.

Narrator: Meanwhile, Jesus called out to them from shore.

Jesus: John! James! Come with me. You will become fishers of people, not fish.

James: Father, we are going with Jesus.

John: Yes, we must go with him!

Why do you think these men followed Jesus?

What does it mean to be a "fisher of people"?

Third Sunday in Ordinary Time   Years A and B   Matthew 4:12-23
Mark 1:14-20

The Beatitudes

Leader: In his Sermon on the Mount, Jesus tells how people are to live and what their reward in heaven will be. The responses of people in this story are as we should respond to Jesus' teaching.

Narrator: Jesus saw the crowds and went on the mountain to teach them. After he was finished he called on the people to review the meaning of what they had learned. The people said,

First Person: When I depend on God, I belong to God's kingdom and he will bless me.

Second Person: When I am sad, God will give me comfort.

Third Person: When I am humble, everything good on earth will belong to me.

Fourth Person: I want to obey God more than anything. When I do, God will give me what I want.

Fifth Person: I am merciful to other people and because of this God will bless me with mercy.

Sixth Person: My heart is pure. I will see God.

Seventh Person: I am a peacemaker. They call me a child of God.

Eighth Person: I have done what is right yet I have been treated badly. Now I belong to God's kingdom.

Jesus: Yes, you are right. God will bless you when people mistreat you or tell lies about you because you believe in me. Be happy because you will be rewarded in heaven. Remember, the prophets have been treated in the same way.

How do you depend on God?

When was a time God blessed you?

Fourth Sunday in Ordinary Time   Year A   Matthew 5:1-12

You Are the Light of the World

Leader: Jesus tells us that we are the light of the world. The disciples' thoughts shared in this presentation should be like our own thoughts.

Narrator: Addressing the disciples, Jesus said,

Jesus: You are the salt of the earth. But what if salt loses its taste? Then it is not good for anything, and should be thrown out.

First Disciple: Salt is not used by itself, only with other foods. Jesus must mean that I should work with others.

Jesus: You are the light of the world. A city built on a hill cannot be hidden. It is there for everyone to see. No one lights a lamp and then hides it under a basket. The light is put on the table, so that the light can shine on everything.

Second Disciple: He must mean that I should work and care for those who need me the most.

Jesus: Your light must shine with all people so everyone can see the good that you do. Then they too will give glory to God.

How are Christians salt of the earth?

How do your good works shine for everyone to see?

Fifth Sunday in Ordinary Time   Year A   Matthew 5:13-16

Jesus Fulfills the Commandments

Leader: In a continuation of the Sermon on the Mount, Jesus speaks to us and tells how he has come to complete the law of Moses, not abolish it.

Jesus: I have not come to do away with the law of Moses and the prophets. I have come to complete what they have said. Whoever breaks the commandments will be the least important in heaven. Whoever obeys the laws and teaches others to obey them will be great in heaven. You must be holier than the teachers of the law and the Pharisees or you will not enter heaven.

First Disciple: But how can I be holier than a teacher of the law?

Jesus: You have heard the commandment,

Voice of God: You shall not kill.

Jesus: I tell you that everyone who gets angry with another will face judgment for that. They will have to be judged by the court, and if the court says the person is guilty, the punishment may be the great fire. If you are bringing a gift to the altar and remember on the way that you have a disagreement with someone else, leave your gift at the altar and go to that person.

Second Disciple: What should I say to that person?

Jesus: Make peace with him or her and then come back and offer your gift to God. If you must go to court over a disagreement, settle it before you go. Otherwise, the other person might give you to the judge, who will hand you to the guard, who will throw you in prison. You will not be released until you pay every penny you owe. Remember, also, God's commandment,

Voice of God: You shall not commit adultery.

Jesus: I say that anyone who looks at another woman with evil on his mind commits adultery. You have also heard the commandment,

Voice of God: Do not use the name of the Lord to make a promise.

Jesus: I say to you, do not swear at all. Heaven is God's throne, so you cannot swear by heaven. Earth is God's footstool, so you cannot swear by earth. Jerusalem is the city of the great king, so you cannot swear by it either. Do not swear by your own head because you cannot even make one hair on your head black or white. Say "yes" when you mean "yes" and "no" when you mean "no."

How many of the Ten Commandments can you name?

Did Jesus make the commandments harder or easier to follow?

Sixth Sunday in Ordinary Time   Year A   Matthew 5:17-37

49

Turn the Other Cheek

Leader: In the Sermon on the Mount, Jesus expands on the commandments and tells his disciples more about the spirit of God's law.

Jesus: You have heard God's commandment,

Voice of God: An eye for an eye, a tooth for a tooth.

Jesus: But I tell you do not try to get even with someone who has hurt you. If someone slaps your right cheek, let the person slap your left cheek too. If anyone wants to take you to court over your shirt, give them your coat, too.

First Disciple: Does this mean I should always do more for people than what they ask?

Jesus: If someone asks you to go a mile for them, go two miles. If someone begs from you, give them what they want. If someone wants to borrow something from you, lend it to them. You have heard God's commandment,

Voice of God: Love your neighbor but hate your enemy.

Jesus: I say love your enemies and pray for anyone who mistreats you. This will prove you are children of God. God causes the sun to rise on good people and bad people. He has the rain fall on both the honest and dishonest.

Second Disciple: What about bad people? Do I have to love them too?

Jesus: What does it prove if you only love the people who love you? Even tax collectors do that. What does it prove if you only speak to your friends? Even unbelievers do that. You must be perfect like your Father in heaven.

How is Jesus' commandment different from "an eye for an eye, a tooth for a tooth"?

What do you find hard about being nice to an enemy?

Seventh Sunday in Ordinary Time   Year A   Matthew 5:38-48

Don't Worry About Your Life

Leader: In today's gospel, Jesus is speaking to his disciples. He tells them not to worry about things like what they will eat or drink or what they will wear.

Jesus: No man can serve two masters. He will either like one more than the other or pay attention to one and hate the other. You cannot serve both God and money. So I tell you, do not worry about your life. Do not worry about what you are going to eat or drink or wear. Life is more than food. Your body is worth more than the clothes you wear.

First Disciple: But I must be secure. How will I have enough to eat and drink?

Jesus: Look at the birds in the sky. They do not plant seed or harvest the grain. They don't even store grain for when they might need it. Your father in heaven takes care of these birds and makes sure they have enough to eat. Aren't you worth more than the birds?

Second Disciple: Yes, I know I am. But it is so hard not to worry about where I will get the material things I will need.

Jesus: It will not help to worry about anything. Why should you worry about clothes to wear? Look at the flowers. They do not work, but even a king like Solomon was not dressed as beautifully as the flowers you see. The plants in the field are grown today and burned tomorrow, but God takes care of them. If he does that for plants, won't he take care of you?

Third Disciple: Maybe God won't take care of me.

Jesus: You should have more faith! Don't worry about if you will have enough food to eat or water to drink or clothes to wear. Everyone, even the unbelievers, worry about those things. Your Father in heaven knows what you need. First, do what you know will please God, and God will give you what you need. Do not worry about tomorrow, because tomorrow will take care of itself. You need to think about today.

What do you worry about?

How do you know God will take care of you?

Eighth Sunday in Ordinary Time   Year A   Matthew 6:24-34

Build Your House on a Rock

Leader: The message of today's gospel is that a wise person lays the foundation of his or her house on rock, not sand. Likewise, the foundation of our own lives must be strongly rooted so as to not blow away.

Jesus: Not everyone who calls me Lord will enter heaven.

First Disciple: How then can we enter heaven, Jesus?

Jesus: Only those who please my Father will enter heaven. On the day of judgment, many will say to me,

Offstage Voice: I called you Lord. I told others about you. I worked miracles and drove away evil spirits, all in your name.

Jesus: And I will say to you, "I do not know you. Get out of my sight, you evil person." Anyone who hears what I am saying and does what I say is very wise.

Second Disciple: I want to do what you say. Lord, teach me how.

Jesus: The wise builder builds his house on rock. When the heavy rains come, the water and strong winds blow against his house, but it does not collapse because it is built on rock. Anyone who hears what I am saying and does not do what I say is very foolish. The foolish one builds a house on sand. When the heavy rains come, the water and strong winds blow against the house, and it falls in and is ruined.

What does Jesus say we have to do in order to go to heaven?

How strong is your faith? Is it built more on sand or rock?

Ninth Sunday in Ordinary Time   Year A   Matthew 7:21-27

Jesus Came to Call Sinners

Leader: Today's gospel reminds us that Jesus did not come only to call those who are just. He also came to call sinners.

Narrator: As Jesus was walking, he saw Matthew, a tax collector, sitting by the custom house.

Jesus: Matthew, come with me.

Matthew: Please bring your disciples and share dinner with me.

Narrator: When Jesus was at dinner with Matthew, a number of tax collectors and sinners dropped by. The Pharisees were close by to observe. One of them said to Jesus' disciples,

Pharisee: I see that Jesus is eating with tax collectors and sinners. Why would Jesus want to eat with people who sin?

Narrator: Jesus overheard this comment and responded,

Jesus: If you are healthy you do not need a doctor. If you are sick, you do need a doctor. Go and study the scriptures. They say, "I would rather you show other people mercy than offer sacrifices." I came not to call only on the just, but sinners too.

Why was it surprising that Jesus called Matthew, a tax collector, to follow him?

Who does Jesus mean by the healthy? the sick? Who is the doctor?

Tenth Sunday in Ordinary Time   Year A   Matthew 9:9-13

The Harvest Is Good

Leader: Jesus called his disciples together and then sent them out to the world.

Narrator: Jesus and his disciples were gathered near a large crowd. Jesus said,

Jesus: Look at this crowd of people. They are so dejected. I feel sorry for them. They are like sheep without a shepherd to take care of them.

Narrator: Jesus then directed his next comments to his disciples.

Jesus: There is a large crop in the field that must be harvested and there are not enough workers. Ask the one in charge of the harvest to send out more workers. I am sending my twelve disciples to help.

Peter: I will help, Lord. Will you, Andrew?

Andrew: You know I will, Peter. I will do whatever the Lord wants me to do. What about you, James?

James: I will go wherever the Lord wants me to go. John, what about you and the others?

John: Here are Philip, Bartholomew, Thomas, Matthew, James, Thaddeus, Simon the Zealot, and Judas Iscariot. We will all go.

Jesus: Do not go to the Gentiles or to any Samaritan town. I want you to find the lost sheep of Israel. Wherever you go, tell everyone that the kingdom of God is near. Heal the sick, raise the dead, cure the lepers, and send out demons. You have been given a gift and you must give that gift to others.

Who is the one in charge of the harvest? Who are the workers?

What does God want you to do with your gifts?

Eleventh Sunday in Ordinary Time   Year A   Matthew 9:36–10:8

Do Not Be Afraid

Leader: Jesus instructs his disciples to not be afraid. He tells them not to fear those who can kill the body but not kill the soul.

Jesus: You must not be afraid of anyone! Everything that is hidden will be uncovered and every secret will be known. I tell you these things in darkness and you must tell them in the day. I whisper these things to you and you must shout them from the rooftops. Don't be afraid of people who can kill your body.

First Disciple: Why shouldn't I be afraid of people who can hurt me and kill me?

Jesus: They cannot hurt your soul. You should fear God because he is the one who can destroy your body and your soul in hell. Your Father knows all. Two sparrows are not worth very much money, but your Father in heaven knows if one of them falls to the ground.

Second Disciple: Does God care for me that much?

Jesus: Your Father in heaven knows how many hairs are on your head. Don't be afraid. You are worth so much more than hundreds of sparrows. If you tell other people that you are my follower, I will vouch for you in heaven before my Father. If you deny that you are my follower, I will deny you to my Father in heaven.

Who or what makes you afraid?

How can you tell that God loves you?

Twelfth Sunday in Ordinary Time   Year A   Matthew 10:26-33

Lose Your Life for the Gospel

Leader: In today's gospel, Jesus explains both the difficulties and the rewards of being his follower.

Narrator: Jesus was speaking with his apostles. He told them,

Jesus: You must love me more than your father or mother or son or daughter, or you cannot be called my disciple. You must take up your cross and follow me, or you cannot be called my disciple.

First Disciple: I have given up everything to follow you, Lord.

Jesus: If your desires are more important to you than me, you will lose your life. If I am more important to you than your desires, you will save your life.

Second Disciple: How will we be able to recognize your followers?

Jesus: Whoever welcomes you, welcomes me. Whoever welcomes me, welcomes the one who sent me. Anyone who welcomes a prophet, just because that person is a prophet, will receive the same reward as a prophet. Whoever welcomes a holy person, just because that person is holy, will receive the same reward as a holy person. Anyone who gives one of my disciples even a cool drink of water, just because that person is my disciple, will be rewarded.

Jesus says we must put him first, even before our parents and families. How can you do that?

What can you do to welcome Jesus?

Thirteenth Sunday in Ordinary Time   Year A   Matthew 10:37-42

Come to Me

Leader: In today's gospel, Jesus says, "Shoulder my yoke . . . for my yoke is easy and my burden light." A yoke is a harness worn by oxen and work horses. When wearing a yoke, the animals must obey and work hard. Oppositely, God's peace that Jesus offers lightens our burdens and gives our lives deep meaning.

Jesus: Father, you are Lord of heaven and earth. Thank you for hiding the truth from the wise and clever people and showing the truth to ordinary people. You did this because this is what pleases you.

First Disciple: We have so much to learn about God. Tell us about the Father.

Jesus: Everything I have is from the Father and he is the only one who truly knows the Son. The only one who truly knows the Son is the Father. And now the Son wants to tell everyone about the Father so that they will know him, too.

Second Disciple: Life is so hard, Jesus. What can give my soul rest?

Jesus: Come to me if you are tired and have heavy burdens or problems. I will give you rest. Take my yoke on your shoulders and you will learn from me. I am gentle and my heart is humble. You will find rest with me. My yoke is easy and my burden is light.

Why do you think God hides the truth from those who think they are wise and clever?

How does Jesus make our lives easier?

Fourteenth Sunday in Ordinary Time   Year A   Matthew 11:25-30

Parable of the Sower

Leader: When Jesus taught the crowds, he often used parables or stories to help explain the message. This helped the people understand his teachings.

Narrator: Jesus left the house and went to the lakeside to teach the crowds. The crowd was so large that he got into a boat so that everyone could see him.

Jesus: I want to tell you a story about a farmer planting seeds. The farmer said,

Farmer: I have scattered a lot of seeds. Some of it landed on the road, and the birds ate it. Some of it fell on rocky ground. It started to grow real fast, but when the sun came up it was too hot for the plants and they died because they did not have deep roots. Some of the seed fell with the thornbushes and they smothered the plants. But a few seeds landed on good soil and the plants produced very well.

Jesus: Listen, anyone with ears!

First Disciple: Why do you always teach the crowd with stories?

Jesus: I have not taught everyone about the secrets of heaven, only you. Whoever has something will be given more. Whoever has only a little will lose even that. I use stories when I talk to the others because they look but they do not see and they hear but they do not listen or understand. Remember, the prophet Isaiah said,

Voice of Isaiah: These people will listen but not understand, they will look but not see. They are stubborn people. If they could see or understand, they would come to me and I would heal them.

Jesus: But God has blessed you, my disciples. You do see with your eyes and hear with your ears. There have been many prophets in the past who wanted to hear and see what you have, but they did not.

Second Disciple: Please teacher, explain the parable of the farmer to us.

Jesus: The seeds that fell on the road are the people who hear God's message about heaven but do not understand it. The evil one comes and takes the message from their hearts. The seeds that fell on rocky ground are people who hear the message and are happy and accept the message right away. But they don't have deep roots, and their faith does not last long. They give up if life gets hard. The seeds that fall with the thornbushes are the people who hear the message, but the message gets choked by life's worries. The seeds that fall on good ground are the people who hear and understand the message and put it to good use, multiplying it in every way.

Why did Jesus teach in parables?

What does Jesus expect from you if you are good seed?

Fifteenth Sunday in Ordinary Time   Year A   Matthew 13:1-23

Weeds Among Wheat

Leader: In today's gospel, Jesus uses parables to help us understand what God's kingdom is like.

Narrator: Speaking before the crowds, Jesus said,

Jesus: The kingdom of heaven is like what happened when a farmer planted good seed in a field. The enemies came in the night and planted bad seeds among the good seeds. When the seeds sprouted the farmer and servants noticed what happened. They talked about it.

Servant: Sir, there are weeds among your crop. Do you want us to go out in the field and pull up all the weeds?

First Farmer: No, because you might pull up the wheat too. Leave the weeds alone for now. When we harvest the wheat, I will tell the workers to collect the weeds and burn them. And they will put the wheat in the barn.

Narrator: Jesus continued with other parables to explain God's kingdom. He said,

Jesus: The kingdom of heaven is also like what happens when a farmer plants a mustard seed. The farmer says to himself,

Second Farmer: This mustard seed is a very small seed, but it will make a plant as big as a tree when full grown. The birds will come and makes nests in its branches.

Jesus: The kingdom of heaven is also like what happens when yeast is mixed with flour. All the dough will rise.

Narrator: Then leaving the crowds, Jesus met alone with his disciples. One of them said,

Disciple: Teacher, explain what the story about the weeds in the fields means.

Jesus: It was the Son of Man who planted the good seed. The field is the whole world and the good seeds are the people who belong to God's kingdom. The bad seeds are the people who belong to the devil. The harvest time is the judgment day and the workers who bring in the harvest are the angels. At the end of time, the Son of Man will send his angels to gather the weeds and burn them. The angels will gather anyone who sins or causes others to sin and throw them in the burning furnace where they will cry out in pain. But everyone who has lived a good life will shine like the sun in God's kingdom. Now pay attention to what I have said.

How is God like a farmer?

How are we like seeds?

Sixteenth Sunday in Ordinary Time   Year A   Matthew 13:24-43

The Kingdom Is Like . . .

Leader: In today's gospel, Jesus teaches us about the kingdom of heaven.

Jesus: The kingdom of heaven is like someone who finds buried treasure. The person says,

Person: I have found this treasure buried in the field. I will hide the treasure and go and sell everything I have. I will use that money to buy this field. Then the treasure will be mine.

Jesus: Or, the kingdom of heaven is like a shop owner who has found a great pearl. The shop owner says,

Shop Owner: What a valuable pearl I have discovered. I will sell everything that I own and use the money to buy this pearl.

Jesus: And, the kingdom of heaven is like what happens when fishermen have a net filled with fish.

First Fisherman: Let's take this net full of fish to shore.

Second Fisherman: We'll separate the good fish from the bad fish, and throw the bad fish away.

Jesus: That's how it will be at the end of time. The angels will come and separate the good people from the evil people. The evil people will be thrown into the flames where they will cry out in pain. Do you understand what I am telling you?

Disciple: Yes, we understand.

Jesus: Anyone who studies the scriptures and becomes a disciple of the kingdom of heaven is someone who has brought out of storage both new and old treasures.

How valuable is God's kingdom?

What will happen at the end of time?

Seventeenth Sunday in Ordinary Time   Year A   Matthew 13:44-52

Feeding of the Multitude

Leader: No matter where Jesus went a large crowd continued to follow.

Narrator: Jesus climbed the hillside and sat down with his disciples. This happened shortly before Passover. A disciple said,

First Disciple: Jesus, the people are coming up here, too. There are thousands of them.

Jesus: How shall we feed all these people? Where can we buy enough bread for them to eat?

Second Disciple: Jesus, it would take almost a year's wages to buy that much bread.

Third Disciple: There is a boy here who has five loaves of bread and a few dried fish. But what good will that do for so many people?

Jesus: Tell the people to sit down. Tell the boy to come here.

Boy: I don't have enough for everyone, but you can have what I do have.

Narrator: Jesus took the bread and said,

Jesus: Thank you God for this bread. Give this to the people to eat. Here is the fish. Give this to everyone.

Fourth Disciple: Jesus, everyone is eating bread and fish. They have all had plenty to eat and there is some left over.

Jesus: Gather up the leftover food so it doesn't get wasted.

Fifth Disciple: There are twelve baskets of food here after everyone has had their fill. How can that be from five loaves and two fish?

Person in the Crowd: Did you see what Jesus did? He must be the prophet we have been waiting for. He must be the Messiah.

Jesus: I must leave and go up the mountain alone. I am afraid they will try to make me their king.

Why did Jesus ask his disciples "How shall we feed all these people?" if he knew what would happen?

What kind of king do you think the people would want Jesus to be?

Eighteenth Sunday in Ordinary Time   Year A   Matthew 14:13-21

Walking on Water

Leader: After the feeding of the thousands, Jesus sent his disciples off to the other side of the lake while he stayed back. After he did this he went up into the hills by himself to pray.

Narrator: The disciples were in the boat a long way from shore.

First Disciple: The boat is going against the wind and the waves are getting high.

Second Disciple: Look! On the water! It looks like someone is walking toward us on the water.

Third Disciple: Is it a ghost? What is it? I'm scared.

Jesus: Courage! Don't be afraid. It's me, Jesus.

Peter: If you are really Jesus, tell me to come across the water to you.

Jesus: Peter, come!

Narrator: Peter got out of the boat and started walking toward Jesus across the water.

First Disciple: Look! Peter's doing it. He's walking on water too!

Peter: The wind is so strong. I am afraid! I'm sinking now. Save me, Lord.

Jesus: Here, take my hand! Where is your faith? Why did you not believe?

Narrator: As they got into the boat, the heavy winds and surf calmed down. The disciples bowed down before him and said,

Second Disciple: You really are the Son of God.

How would you have felt if you saw Jesus walking toward you on water?

Why do you think Peter got out of the boat? Why do you think he started to sink?

Nineteenth Sunday in Ordinary Time   Year A   Matthew 14:22-33

A Woman of Faith

Leader: In today's gospel, Jesus encounters a woman with great faith.

Narrator: Jesus was in the area of Tyre and Sidon. A woman from Canaan came to him. She was not a Jewish woman and the disciples did not want her to bother Jesus. Nevertheless, she started shouting,

Woman: Lord, Son of David, have pity on me and help me! My daughter has evil spirits.

Narrator: Jesus did not speak to the woman. And his disciples pleaded with him,

First Disciple: Jesus, tell that woman to go away.

Second Disciple: She keeps following us and shouting at you.

Third Disciple: Yes, make her go away.

Jesus: I was sent to help the lost sheep of the people of Israel.

Narrator: But the woman had come up to Jesus and was now kneeling at his feet.

Woman: Please, help me Lord.

Jesus: It is not fair to help you. It would be like taking food from children and feeding it to dogs.

Woman: But even dogs get the crumbs from under the table.

Jesus: Woman, you have a lot of faith. You will be given what you want.

Narrator: At that moment, her daughter was cured.

Who did Jesus come to serve?

What did Jesus mean when he said helping the woman would be like taking good food from children and feeding it to the dogs?

Twentieth Sunday in Ordinary Time　　　　Year A　　　　Matthew 15:21-28

Who Do You Say That I Am?

Leader: In today's gospel, Peter correctly names Jesus' identity. To Peter, Jesus gives the keys of the kingdom.

Narrator: Jesus and his disciples were traveling near the town of Caesarea Philippi.

Jesus: What are people saying about the Son of Man?

First Disciple: Some people are saying that you are John the Baptist.

Second Disciple: Some people are saying that you are the prophet Elijah.

Third Disciple: Some people are saying that you are the prophet Jeremiah, or another prophet.

Jesus: But, you? Who do you say that I am?

Simon Peter: You are the Messiah, the Son of the living God.

Jesus: You are blessed, Simon, son of Jonah. You know this because my Father in heaven showed you. I will call you Peter, which means "rock," and on this rock I will build my church. Death will have no power over my church. I will give you the keys of heaven. God in heaven will allow whatever you allow on earth, and he will not allow anything you do not allow.

Narrator: Jesus then gave the disciples strict orders not to tell anyone that he was the Messiah.

How did Peter know Jesus was the Messiah, the Son of the living God?

What does it mean to say that Peter has the keys of the kingdom?

Twenty-First Sunday in Ordinary Time　　　Year A　　　　　Matthew 16:13-20

Discipleship

Leader: Jesus tells us that if we wish to follow him, we must be willing to give up everything else.

Narrator: Jesus made it clear what was going to happen to him.

Jesus: Soon I will go to Jerusalem. The leaders of the nation, the chief priests, and the teachers of the law of Moses will hurt me and cause me to suffer. I will be put to death, but I will rise to life after three days.

Narrator: Peter began to argue with Jesus.

Peter: Jesus, don't say such things. That kind of thing must never happen to you.

Jesus: Get away from me, you Satan. You are not thinking like God, you are thinking like everyone else.

Narrator: Then Jesus spoke to the other disciples.

Jesus: If you want to follow me, you must give up everything else. You must forget about yourself. If you just want to save your own life, you will lose your life. If you give up your life for me, you will have life. What good would it be if you owned the whole world, but destroyed your own soul? What would you be willing to give to get your soul back? Soon, the Son of Man will come with his angels, in the glory of the Father in heaven, and reward all those who have behaved well.

Why was Jesus angry with Peter?

How do you respond to Jesus' question, "What good would it be if you owned the whole world but destroyed your own soul?"

Twenty-Second Sunday in Ordinary Time   Year A   Matthew 16:21-27

The Power of Forgiveness

Leader: Today's gospel reminds us that Jesus has given us the power to forgive one another.

Jesus: I will tell you how to work out a disagreement. Follow this example:

First Person: My neighbor has offended me. I will go to my neighbor and talk about it. I won't mention the problem to anyone else. If we can work out an agreement, I have won back a follower who was lost. *(speaking to second person)* I'd like to talk to you about what you did to me.

Second Person: Leave me alone. I didn't do anything wrong to you.

First Person: I will be back with some witnesses. They will listen to both sides and see who is right and who is wrong.

Jesus: If the person does not listen even to the witnesses, tell the leaders of the church. If the follower does not listen to the church officials, he must be treated as someone you do not trust. I promise you that if you forgive something on earth, God will forgive it in heaven. If you do not forgive it on earth, God will not forgive it in heaven. I promise you that if two people on earth pray for the same thing, God will give it to you. Whenever two or three of you come together in my name, I am with you.

What are the steps Jesus gives for working out a disagreement?

When does Jesus say he is with us?

Twenty-Third Sunday in Ordinary Time   Year A   Matthew 18:15-20

How Many Times Should We Forgive?

Leader: How many times should we forgive others? Today's gospel tells us not seven times, but as many times as is necessary.

Narrator: Peter approached Jesus with this question:

Peter: Jesus, tell me. How many times should I forgive someone who has done something wrong? Should I forgive as often as seven times?

Jesus: No! Not seven times, but seventy-seven times. Let me tell you what the kingdom of heaven is like. It's like this king who decides to settle accounts with some of his servants. The king says,

King: I want to know how much everyone owes me. Bring me my servants.

First Servant: King, I owe you ten thousand silver coins, but I can't pay you back.

King: Then I will sell you and your wife and children and everything you own.

First Servant (crying): Have mercy on me. I will pay you eventually.

King: Oh, stop crying. You are making me feel bad. I will not sell you or your wife or your children or your possessions. And, you don't have to pay me back.

Jesus: Now on the way out the servant met a second servant who owed him one hundred denari, barely one day's pay. The first servant began to choke him.

First Servant: Pay me back what you owe me!

Second Servant (begging): Please! Have mercy on me and I will pay you back.

First Servant: I have no pity. I will put you in jail, until you pay what you owe.

Jesus: After the second servant was put in jail, his fellow servants told the king what happened. The king had the first servant brought before him.

King: You are evil! When you begged me for mercy, I felt sorry for you and said you did not have to pay me back. But when this other man begged for your mercy, you did not feel sorry for him. You put him in jail! So now I will put you in jail and they will torture you until you pay back every bit of the money you owe me.

Jesus: And that is how the Father will deal with you unless you forgive others from your heart.

What do you find hard about forgiving others?

How many times should you forgive a person for the same offense?

Twenty-Fourth Sunday in Ordinary Time   Year A   Matthew 18:21-35

The Workers in the Vineyard

Leader: Jesus used parables to help explain what the kingdom of God is like.

Jesus: This is what the kingdom of heaven will be like. A landowner went out at daybreak to hire some workers.

Owner: I have this vineyard and I need some workers to pick the grapes.

First Worker: I will pick your grapes. It is early in the morning and I will work until evening. How much will you pay me?

Owner: I will pay you for a day's work.

Jesus: The first worker and his companions went out and began to harvest the grapes. About three hours later the owner went out and found other workers. Then, in the same way, he went out again three hours after that and found still more workers and told them he would pay them what was fair. Then, even though the day was almost over, still more laborers were needed. The owner went out again.

Owner: It's five o'clock in the afternoon. Why aren't you working?

Second Worker: No one has hired me.

Owner: I will hire you. Go to work in my vineyard and I will pay you what is fair.

Jesus: At the end of the day, the owner called in all the workers for their pay.

Owner: I will start with the workers I hired at five o'clock. Here's a full day's pay.

Jesus: Then he called the workers that he hired at three o'clock, and at noon, and at nine o'clock in the morning.

Owner: You have all worked very hard. I will pay you a full day's pay. Now for those who began first thing in the morning. I will pay you a full day's pay.

First Worker: But we have worked longer than anyone else. We should be paid more than the others who only worked part of a day.

Owner: I did not cheat you. I paid you what we agreed on. It is none of your business if I want to pay the other workers the same as you. You should not be jealous.

Jesus: This is how it is in heaven. Everyone who is first will be last and everyone who is last will be first.

Was it fair to pay the other workers the same as the first workers were paid?

What did Jesus mean, "That is how it is in heaven"?

Twenty-Fifth Sunday in Ordinary Time　　　Year A　　　　　　　Matthew 20:1-16

The Parable of Two Sons

Leader: Once more, today's gospel has a surprising message: sinners will enter the kingdom of heaven before some who consider themselves to be holy.

Narrator: Jesus said to the chief priests and other religious leaders,

Jesus: I want to tell you a story about two sons. The father said to both sons,

Father: I want both of you to go the vineyard and work today.

Jesus: The older brother answered,

Older Son: No, I have other things to do today. I am not going to work in the vineyard.

Jesus: But the younger son said,

Younger Son: I will go and work in the vineyard today.

Jesus: But later, they both changed their minds.

Older Son: I told my father I wouldn't go to work today, but I know he needs help. I will go and do what my father has asked me to do.

Younger Son: I know I told my father I would go and work, but I really don't want to. I'll go another day and work.

Jesus: Which of the sons obeyed the father?

Chief Priest: The older son obeyed the father.

Jesus: You can be sure that the worst sinners will get into heaven before you do! John the Baptist came to show you how to live the right way, but you would not believe him. Sinners did believe him. And even when you saw what they did and knew they must be right, you would not change your mind.

_____

Why was what the older son did right and what the younger son did wrong?

What did Jesus mean when he said "Sinners will get into heaven before you do"?

Twenty-Sixth Sunday in Ordinary Time   Year A   Matthew 21:28-32

The Parable of the Tenants

Leader: Jesus came to share the good news with the Chosen People, the Jews. When some of the Chosen People did not listen to his words, Jesus began to share the good news with non-Jews, called Gentiles.

Jesus: There was a property owner who planted a vineyard.

Owner: I have worked hard to prepare this land. I have planted the grapevines and built a wall and added many other features around the property. Now I am leaving the country for a while, so I will rent this vineyard to tenants. They can care for the grapes and pick them for me. I will return at harvest to collect my share.

Jesus: The property owner returned to find the tenants harvesting the grapes.

Owner: Slaves, go to the tenants to get my share of the profits.

First Slave: Sir, we tried to do that. The tenants beat me up, they killed another slave, and stoned a third. The tenants will not give you your share.

Owner: I will send more slaves to collect my share of the profits.

Second Slave: Sir, we tried. But the tenants have killed more of us.

Owner: Very well. I will send my son. Surely they will respect him and give him all that they owe me.

Jesus: The owner's son went to visit the tenants.

First Tenant: This is the one who will inherit everything.

Second Tenant: Let's kill him. Then we can have everything that is his.

Jesus: The tenants threw the man's son out of the vineyard and killed him too. What do you think the property owner will do to those tenants?

Narrator: One of the elders answered,

Elder: He will bring those wretches to an end. Then he will rent out his vineyard to other tenants who will give him his share of the profits at harvest time.

Jesus: You know what the scripture says, "The stone which the builders rejected has become the cornerstone. The Lord did this marvelous deed." I tell you then, God will give his kingdom to people who will produce good fruit.

How is the parable Jesus told like his own life?

How do you produce good fruit for God's kingdom?

Twenty-Seventh Sunday in Ordinary Time   Year A   Matthew 21:33-43

The Parable of the Wedding Feast

Leader: Jesus told parables to help explain what the kingdom of heaven is like. In the parable of the wedding feast, Jesus tells us that many are invited but few are actually chosen for God's kingdom.

Narrator: Jesus told this parable to the chief priests and elders of the Jewish people.

Jesus: The kingdom of heaven is like a king who gave a great feast for his son's wedding. The king said,

King: I have prepared a great wedding feast for my son and his bride. Go and call those who have been invited.

First Servant: My master has prepared a great feast for his son and his son's new bride. He invites you to come.

First Guest: I have to work. I can't come.

Second Guest: I have to take care of my farm. I won't be there.

Third Guest: I don't want to go. I will kill this servant so he can't tell the king that I don't want to be there.

King: I have invited several people to my son's wedding, but they won't come. Go and burn their city! They were invited but they don't deserve to come. Now go out on the streets and invite everyone you see.

Second Servant: Come one and come all! The king has prepared a feast and you are invited.

Jesus: The banquet room was filled with guests, some good and some bad. Then the king saw one guest who was not dressed properly.

King: Why do you come to my son's wedding feast dressed like that? (to the servants) Take this man and tie his hands and feet and throw him out into the night. He will cry and grit his teeth in pain.

Jesus: For many are invited, but only a few are chosen.

How do you think a wedding feast is like the kingdom of heaven?

What does Jesus mean, "For many are invited, but only a few are chosen"?

Twenty-Eighth Sunday in Ordinary Time   Year A   Matthew 22:1-14

Paying Taxes to the Emperor

Leader: The Pharisees tried to trick Jesus into saying something against the Roman government, so they could bring him to trial. Jesus knew what they were trying to do and gave them an answer that kept them from trying to trick him again.

First Pharisee: We need to trick Jesus.

Second Pharisee: Let's get him to say something against Caesar, the Roman emperor.

Third Pharisee: Teacher, we know you are honest and will tell the truth. You teach people about God and what God wants people to do.

Fourth Pharisee: You treat everyone the same, no matter who they are. What do you think? Should we pay taxes to Caesar or not?

Jesus: Why are you trying to trick me? Show me the coin that you use to pay taxes with.

First Pharisee: Here is a coin.

Jesus: Whose picture do you see on the coin?

Second Pharisee: It is Caesar's head.

Jesus: Well, then, give back to Caesar what belongs to Caesar and give to God what belongs to God.

Why were the Pharisees trying to trick Jesus?

According to the gospel, what belongs to Caesar and what belongs to God?

Twenty-Ninth Sunday in Ordinary Time   Year A   Matthew 22:15-21

The Great Commandment

Leader: In today's gospel we hear the Great Commandment: you shall love God and you shall love your neighbor as yourself.

Narrator: When the Pharisees heard that Jesus could not be tricked by the Sadducees, they themselves tried to catch him off guard again.

First Pharisee: Let's try to trap Jesus in his words.

Second Pharisee: We have to get him to say something against God.

Third Pharisee: Then everyone will know that we are right.

Fourth Pharisee: Teacher, which commandment is the greatest?

Jesus: You shall love the Lord your God with all your heart, soul, and mind. This is the most important of all commandments. The second is like it: you shall love your neighbor as yourself.

How can you love God with all your heart and soul and mind?

How can you love your neighbor as yourself?

Thirtieth Sunday in Ordinary Time   Year A   Matthew 22:34-40

Humble Yourself

Leader: In today's gospel Jesus criticizes those who attract attention to themselves and he reminds us that we must always practice what we preach.

Narrator: Addressing the people and his disciples, Jesus said,

Jesus: The Pharisees and teachers know the law of Moses. Do what they teach you to do, but don't follow their example. They say one thing and do another. This is how they act,

First Pharisee: You there! Carry all of this load over for me.

Jesus: Or,

Second Pharisee: Look at how good I am. I wear the holy scripture dangling from ribbons on my clothing.

Jesus: And when they go to banquets or the synagogue they always say,

Third Pharisee: Seat me in the front.

Jesus: When anyone greets them, they tell the person,

Fourth Pharisee: You must call me teacher.

Jesus: But no one should be called teacher. There is only one teacher and you are all brothers and sisters. All of you have the same Father in heaven. The Messiah is your only teacher. Don't call anyone on earth your father or your teacher. Whoever is greatest among you should be the servant to others. If you put yourself above other people, you will be made lower than them. If you put yourself lower than other people, you will be honored.

What does it mean to practice what you preach?

If you want to be great what does Jesus say you should do?

Thirty-First Sunday in Ordinary Time   Year A   Matthew 23:1-12

The Parable of the Ten Bridesmaids

Leader: In today's gospel Jesus tells us to always be ready because we don't know when the Lord is coming.

Jesus: The kingdom of heaven is like this: There were ten bridesmaids who went to a wedding feast for the groom. They had oil-burning lamps to light their way. Five were foolish and five were wise.

First Foolish Bridesmaid: I have my lamp, but no oil. Oh well, I'll get my oil later. There is plenty of time.

First Wise Bridesmaid: I have my lamp and it has plenty of oil. I even have extra oil in case I have to wait for the groom for a long time.

Second Foolish Bridesmaid: Where is the groom? I thought he would be here.

Third Foolish Bridesmaid: I'm getting tired. I'm going to sleep for awhile.

Second Wise Bridesmaid: Here he comes! Here comes the groom.

Third Wise Bridesmaid: Bring your lamps to light his way. Come and meet him!

Fourth Foolish Bridesmaid: I don't have enough oil. My lamp won't light.

Fifth Foolish Bridesmaid: Could we have some of your oil so our lamps will light?

Fourth Wise Bridesmaid: There is not enough oil for everyone.

Fifth Wise Bridesmaid: Go and buy your own oil for your lamps.

First Foolish Bridesmaid: Let's go and buy our oil.

Second Foolish Bridesmaid: We had better hurry or we'll miss everything.

Jesus: The five foolish bridesmaids went to buy oil for their lamps. In the meantime the groom arrived. The five wise bridesmaids were ready, and went into the wedding feast with him. The foolish bridesmaids arrived later.

Third Foolish Bridesmaid: Sir, please open the door for us!

Groom: I don't even know you. I won't open the door to let you in.

Jesus: So always be ready. You don't know the day or the hour that this will happen.

What should we do to prepare for the Lord?

When should we prepare for the Lord to come again?

Thirty-Second Sunday in Ordinary Time   Year A   Matthew 25:1-13

The Parable of the Talents

Leader: In today's gospel Jesus tells us when we have been faithful in small responsibilities we will be able to enter the kingdom of heaven.

Jesus: The kingdom of heaven is like this: A master gathered his servants together.

Master: I am leaving on a trip. I am leaving you *(to the first servant)* five thousand coins, you *(to the second servant)* two thousand coins, and you *(to the third servant)* one thousand coins.

Servants *(at once)***:** Thank you, Master.

Jesus: The man left the country, trusting that his servants would use the money wisely.

First Servant: I will use these five thousand coins to earn more money for my master.

Second Servant: I will use these two thousand coins to earn more money for my master.

Third Servant: I am afraid of my master because he is cruel. I don't want to lose this money he gave me. I will dig a hole and hide this money until he comes back. Then I can give every penny back to him.

Jesus: Now a long time later, the master of those servants came back.

Master: Servants, come here! What have you done with the money I gave you?

Jesus: The first servant and the second servant told their master that they had earned more money for him and he was very pleased.

Master: I put you in charge of a little but now I will put you in charge of more.

Third Servant: Sir, I buried the money you gave me. You are hard to get along with. I was frightened that you would be mad if I lost your money. Here is all the money you trusted me with.

Master: You are a lazy good for nothing. You should have at least put my money in a bank so I could earn interest. I will take your money and give it to the servants who have more coins. Everyone who has something will be given more. I will take everything away from those who don't have enough. You are a worthless servant. I will throw you out into the night to cry and grind your teeth.

What gifts has God given you?

What are some good things you are doing with your gifts?

Thirty-Third Sunday in Ordinary Time   Year A   Matthew 25:14-30

Christit the King

Leader: Jesus tells us what it will be like at the final judgment. He will sit in glory and separate all people according to their behavior.

Jesus: When the Son of Man comes in his glory, he will be with all of his angels and he will sit on a royal throne. All the people from every nation will be brought before him for judgment. He will separate them as a shepherd separates the sheep from the goats. Sheep! On my right! Goats! On my left!

Narrator: To the sheep Jesus said,

Jesus: My Father has blessed you. Come into heaven. When I was hungry, you gave me food to eat. When I was thirsty, you gave me something to drink. When I was a stranger you welcomed me. When I was naked, you gave me clothes. When I was sick, you took care of me. When I was in jail, you visited me.

First Sheep: When did I give you something to eat?

Second Sheep: When did I give you something to drink?

Third Sheep: When did I welcome you in?

Fourth Sheep: When did I give you clothes to wear?

Fifth Sheep: When did I take care of you?

Sixth Sheep: When did I visit you in jail?

Jesus: Whenever you did it for any of my people, even the lowest ones, you did it to me.

Narrator: To the goats on his left, Jesus said,

Jesus: Get away from me, you are under God's curse. Go into the everlasting fire prepared by the devil and his angels. For I was hungry and you gave me nothing to eat. I was thirsty and you gave me nothing to drink. I was a stranger and you did not welcome me. I was naked and you gave me nothing to wear. I was sick and you did not take care of me. I was in jail and you did not visit me.

First Goat: When did I see you hungry and give you no food?

Second Goat: When did I see you thirsty and give you nothing to drink?

Third Goat: When did I not welcome you?

Fourth Goat: When did I see you naked and give you nothing to wear?

Fifth Goat: When were you sick and I did not take care of you?

Sixth Goat: When were you in jail and I did not visit you?

Jesus: Whenever you failed to help any of my people, you failed to help me.

When do we see Jesus?

What should we do when we see Jesus?

Last Sunday in Ordinary Time   Year A   Matthew 25:31-46

Sunday Gospels

(with Christmas and New Year's Gospels)

Year B

Be Ready!

Leader: Advent is a time of preparation and waiting. Jesus tells us we must always be ready, because we don't know when he will return.

Jesus: Watch out and be ready. You don't know when the time will come. It is like what happens when a person goes away for a while and places his servants in charge of everything. The Master says,

Master: I am going away for a while. You must protect my family and my property. Be on guard and be alert. Be ready when I return. *(Master leaves.)*

First Servant: We really don't know exactly when the master of the house will return.

Second Servant: It could be in the evening or at midnight or before dawn or in the morning.

Third Servant: Don't let him find you asleep.

Fourth Servant: We must all be alert.

What is hard about waiting?

What is hard about waiting for Jesus to return?

First Sunday in Advent   Year B   Mark 13:33-37

I Am Not Worthy to Unfasten His Sandal

Leader: The third Sunday in Advent is a day of hope, represented by our lighting of the pink candle on the Advent wreath. In the gospel today, John the Baptist tells us he is not the Messiah, but he is here to help people prepare for the Messiah, who is coming soon.

Narrator: A prophet named John was sent to tell about God's light and to lead all people to follow the light of faith. John wasn't the light himself. He came only to tell about the light.

First Temple Helper *(to John)*: Who are you?

John the Baptist: Well, I am not the Messiah, if that is what you are asking.

Scribe: Are you Elijah then?

John: No, I am not.

Second Temple Helper: Are you the Prophet?

John: No, I am not.

First Temple Leader: Who are you then? Tell us who you are.

John: I am only someone in the desert shouting, "Get the road ready for the Lord."

Second Temple Leader: Why are you baptizing people if you are not the Messiah, or Elijah, or the Prophet?

John: I use water to baptize. There is one among you that you do not recognize yet. I am not worthy to unfasten his sandal.

Why would people ask John the Baptist these questions?

What does John mean, "I am not worthy to unfasten his sandal"?

Third Sunday in Advent   Year B   John 1:6-8, 19-28

Nothing Is Impossible for God

Leader: Our time of waiting for our Savior is almost over. The Lord is coming!

Narrator: God sent the angel Gabriel to give a message to Mary. Mary was engaged to be married to Joseph, who was from the family of King David.

Angel Gabriel: Mary, you are blessed and the Lord is with you.

Mary: I don't understand. I am afraid. Why do you call me blessed?

Angel Gabriel: Don't be afraid. God is happy with you. You are going to have a son and you will name him Jesus. He will be called the Son of God Most High. God will make him king, like David was. He will rule the people of Israel forever and his kingdom will never end.

Mary: How can I have a son? I am not married.

Angel Gabriel: The Holy Spirit will come down to you and God's power will come over you. Your child will be the Son of God. Elizabeth, your relative, is going to have a baby too. She is old and she thought she would never have any children, but she is going to have a son in three months. Nothing is impossible for God.

Mary: I am the Lord's servant! Let it happen as you have said.

Why was Mary afraid at first?

What did Mary finally decide?

Fourth Sunday in Advent   Year B   Luke 1:26-38

The Presentation

Leader: Today's celebration of the Holy Family reminds us to always keep Jesus central in the lives of our own families.

Narrator: As faithful followers of the law of Moses, Joseph and Mary took their son to be presented at the Temple. According to the law, they brought a pair of turtledoves or two pigeons to offer in sacrifice. At the Temple, Joseph and Mary met a good man named Simeon.

Simeon: I have been waiting for God to save the people of Israel. The Spirit of God came to me and said,

Voice of the Spirit: You will not die until you see God's Chosen One.

Simeon: Mary and Joseph, may I hold your baby? *(He takes Jesus in his arms and looks up to heaven.)* Thank you, God, for keeping your promise to me. I can now die in peace because I have seen what everyone will soon see. I have seen how you will save your people. Not only will the people of Israel be honored, but your power is for all people.

Joseph: Simeon, I am surprised by what you have said.

Simeon: Bless both of you. Mary, this child of yours is a warning for all people. He will be the ruin of some people and the uplifting of others. Mary, you too will suffer. It will be like you have been stabbed with a knife or sword.

Narrator: Anna, an old woman who spent all her days praying and fasting, was also in the Temple.

Anna: I must go and tell everyone about this child, Jesus. We have been praying for Jerusalem to be set free. God has answered our prayers.

Joseph: Mary, we have done what the Law of Moses requires us to do.

Mary: It is time to go home to Nazareth.

Narrator: Jesus grew and became strong and wise, and God blessed him.

What was Simeon waiting for?

How did Simeon's warning to Mary come true?

Holy Family   Year B   Luke 2:22-40

Cleansing of the Temple

Leader: Anger is a normal human feeling. In today's gospel, Jesus is angry at the way his Father's house is being used and he clears the Temple of those who are not there for worship.

Narrator: Since the Passover was near, Jesus and his disciples went up to Jerusalem and entered the Temple area.

Jesus: Why are these people selling cattle and sheep and exchanging their money inside the Temple area?

Narrator: Jesus made a whip out of rope and drove those people out.

Jesus: Get out of here! You have turned my Father's house into a marketplace!

Narrator: One of Jesus' disciples quoted the scriptures.

First Disciple: My love for your house burns in me like a fire.

Second Disciple: Listen! Those words come true in Jesus.

Narrator: Some Jewish leaders spoke out.

Jewish Leader: Why have you destroyed our Temple? You must show us a miracle to prove you were authorized to do this!

Jesus: Destroy this Temple and I will raise it up in three days.

Second Jewish Leader: What! It took forty-six years to build this Temple and you're going to re-build it in three days? I don't think so.

Narrator: Jesus was talking about his body as a Temple. Later, when he was raised from the dead, his disciples remembered what he had said and they believed the scripture and his words. Jesus and his disciples left the Temple.

Third Disciple: Jesus, many people have seen the miracles you have done and they believe you are the Messiah.

Jesus: I know everyone's thoughts. I know who to trust and who not to trust.

Why did Jesus chase the merchants out of the Temple?

What "temple" would Jesus raise up in three days after it was destroyed?

Third Sunday of Lent   Year B   John 2:13-25

The Light Came Into the World

Leader: Today's gospel reminds us that God loved the world so much that he gave his only Son.

Narrator: Jesus spoke to Nicodemus, a Jewish leader.

Jesus: The Son of Man must be lifted up like Moses lifted the metal snake in the desert.

Nicodemus: I know that story. God sent snakes to punish the people of Israel. Then he told Moses to hold a metal snake up on a pole and whoever looked at the snake was cured of their snakebite.

Jesus: Everyone who believes in the Son of Man will have eternal life. God loved this world so much that he sent us his Son. Everyone who believes in him will never really die.

Nicodemus: Why did God send his Son to earth?

Jesus: God sent his Son to save people, not to condemn them. No one who has faith in God's Son will be doomed, but everyone who doesn't believe in God's Son is already cursed. The light came into the world, but the ones who were wicked loved the dark instead of the light. Everyone who does evil hates the light and will not come near it, because they are afraid that others will see what they have done. Everyone who lives a good life will come to the light, and they will let everyone know that God is really the one who is accomplishing all the good that they do.

Why did God send his Son to earth?

What will happen to everyone who lives a good life?

Fourth Sunday of Lent　　　　　Year B　　　　　John 3:14-21

85

A Grain of Wheat Must Die

Leader: Jesus said, "If a grain of wheat falls on the ground and dies, it yields a great harvest." He said this to represent what would happen to him.

Narrator: Jesus knows that his time is short. Still, his disciples fail to understand that he will suffer and die. The Greeks were among those worshipping at the Temple. One Greek person said to the Apostle Philip,

First Greek: Sir, we would like to meet Jesus.

Philip: Andrew, there are some Greeks here who would like to meet Jesus. Let's go ask Jesus if this is okay.

Narrator: Andrew and Philip approached Jesus.

Andrew: Jesus, there are many people who want to see you.

Jesus: The time has come for the Son of Man to be glorified. Everyone knows that even a grain of wheat must die before it can produce more wheat. But if it dies, it will make much more wheat. If you live your life without God, you will lose it. If you live for God in this life, you will be given life forever. If you follow me, you must go with me. If you serve me, my Father will honor you. The time has come for me to suffer. I want to ask my Father to take away this time of pain, but that is why I came into the world. Father, glorify your name!

Voice of God: I have already brought glory to my name and I will do it again!

Second Greek: What was that sound? Was it thunder?

Third Greek: No, I think it was an angel speaking to Jesus!

Jesus: That voice spoke to help you, not me. The time for judgment has come, and the leaders of this world are being thrown out. Once I am lifted up from the earth, all people will want to come to me.

Jesus compares his death to a grain of wheat. What happens to a grain of wheat if you do not plant it? What happens if you do plant it?

Why did Jesus come into this world?

Fifth Sunday of Lent   Year B   John 12:20-33

Peace Be With You

Leader: In today's gospel, the Risen Jesus reminds his disciples that the Christ had to suffer, and that on the third day he would rise from the dead.

Narrator: After Jesus walked with his disciples on the road to Emmaus, his disciples were talking about what happened.

First Disciple: Remember when we were walking to Emmaus and Jesus was with us?

Second Disciple: We didn't recognize him until he broke bread with us and said the blessing.

Narrator: While they were talking about this, Jesus stood among them and said,

Jesus: Peace be with you.

Third Disciple: Are you a ghost?

Jesus: Why would you think I am a ghost? Touch me. A ghost doesn't have flesh and bones like I do.

First Disciple: I am so happy to have you here.

Second Disciple: I can't believe it is really you.

Jesus: Do you have anything to eat?

Third Disciple: Here is some fish we just cooked.

Narrator: Jesus took the fish and ate it before their eyes. Then, he said,

Jesus: Remember when I told you that everything that was written about me in the scriptures had to be fulfilled? Scripture says that the Messiah must suffer and rise from the dead on the third day. People of every nation must be told to turn to God for forgiveness. Begin in Jerusalem and tell everyone what has happened. You are my witnesses.

How did Jesus show the disciples he was not a ghost?

What did Jesus ask his disciples to do?

Third Sunday of Easter   Year B   Luke 24:35-48

The Good Shepherd

Leader: Jesus is the Good Shepherd who watches over his people and saves them, as a shepherd tends his sheep.

Jesus: I am a good shepherd. I will give up my life to save my sheep.

Narrator: Oppositely, hired workers do not care for their sheep in the same way. They say,

First Hired Hand: I am not a shepherd. I do not own these sheep. I have been hired to watch them.

Second Hired Hand: If I see a wolf, I will run away so it won't kill me. The wolf may scatter the sheep so they can't be found or it may kill the sheep. I don't care about the sheep enough to lose my life protecting them from a wolf.

Jesus: I am the Good Shepherd. I know all of my sheep and they know me, too, just like the Father knows me and I know the Father. I will give up my life to save these sheep. I have other sheep that are in another flock. I must take care of them, too, and they will also hear my voice. Then there will be just one flock of sheep and one shepherd. That is why the Father loves me: I will give up my life and take it back again. No one takes my life from me, I give it up of my own free will. I have the power to lay my life down and the power to take it back again. This is what my Father has told me to do.

How is the good shepherd different from hired help?

Why does the Father love Jesus?

Fourth Sunday of Easter   Year B   John 10:11-18

Jesus, the True Vine

Leader: The people of Jesus' time were familiar with large grape vineyards. In today's gospel, Jesus plays on their understanding and describes himself as the vine and his followers as the branches.

Jesus: I am like a grapevine and my Father is like the gardener. He will cut away any branch that does not produce fruit. He will trim the fruitful vines clean so they will produce even more fruit.

First Disciple: How can I be made clean?

Jesus: You, my disciples, are already clean because you have listened to my word. Live on in me and I will live on in you. I am the vine and you are the branches. If we stay together, we can accomplish very much. Without me, you can do nothing. If you do not stay with me, you will be thrown away.

Second Disciple: I want to stay with you, Jesus.

Jesus: If you do not stay with me, you will be like dead branches that are gathered up to be thrown into the fire. Listen to my teachings and let them become part of you.

Third Disciple: I listen to everything you say, Lord.

Jesus: Then you can pray for anything and your prayers will be answered. My Father has been glorified because you became my disciples.

What can a branch do without a vine?

How can you let Jesus' teachings become a part of you?

Fifth Sunday of Easter   Year B   John 15:1-8

Live On in My Love

Leader: Jesus tells us to love one another in the same way that he loves us. The greatest love one can show another is to lay down his or her life for a friend.

Jesus: I have loved you as my Father has loved me. Continue to live in this love.

First Disciple: I will always love you. How can I show you?

Jesus: You will show your love for me by obeying my commandments, just as I showed my love for my Father by obeying his commandments. I have told you this so that you can be completely happy.

Second Disciple: We do obey the commandments of God. What is your commandment?

Jesus: This is my commandment: Love each other as I have loved you.

Third Disciple: How do we love in this way?

Jesus: You are my friends and I would give up my life for you. There is no greater love than that. You are not my slaves, because slaves do not know anything about their masters. You are my friends, because I have told you everything my Father told me.

Fourth Disciple: We chose to follow you, Lord.

Jesus: You did not choose me; I chose you to go out and produce fruit, the kind of fruit that will last forever. The Father will give you everything you ask for, if you ask in my name. Remember, you must love each other.

What is Jesus' commandment?

What did Jesus do for us?

Sixth Sunday of Easter   Year B   John 15:9-17

A Prayer for Jesus' Followers

Leader: Before he died on the cross, Jesus prayed that we, his followers, might be one with him and the Father.

Jesus: Holy Father, I am not in this world anymore, but my followers are still in this world. I ask that you keep them safe, by the power of the name you have given me, so they will be one as we are one.

First Disciple: Why is Jesus praying for us to be safe? We have always been safe with him.

Jesus: I have kept my followers safe while I was here with them. All of my disciples are with me, except the one that had to be lost to carry out the Scriptures.

Second Disciple: Jesus' words are difficult for many to believe in.

Jesus: I am on my way to you, but I say this to show them the way to happiness. I told my disciples your word. There are other people who did not understand your word and they hated my followers because of it.

Third Disciple: What will happen to us?

Jesus: My disciples do not belong in this world any more than I do. I ask that you protect them from the evil one while they are still in this world. I am sending them out into the world with your word, which is truth. I have given myself totally to them, so they belong completely to you.

Why did Jesus say he was not in this world anymore?

What is the way to happiness that Jesus told his disciples?

Seventh Sunday of Easter   Year B   John 17:11-19

Father, Son, and Holy Spirit

Leader: In the Trinity Sunday gospel Jesus gives final instructions to his disciples. Listen for how all three persons in the Holy Trinity are present in this reading.

Narrator: The eleven disciples went to the place where Jesus arranged to meet them.

First Disciple: We must go to the mountain in Galilee.

Second Disciple: Jesus said he would meet us there.

Third Disciple: I don't know what we can expect to see.

Narrator: When they saw Jesus, they fell to their knees. Jesus said,

Jesus: I have command over all of heaven and earth. Go and make disciples of all the nations. Baptize them in the name of the Father, and of the Son, and of the Holy Spirit. Teach them everything I have taught you. I am with you always, even until the end of the world.

What does Jesus want us to do?

When is Jesus with us?

Sunday After Pentecost   Year B   Matthew 28:16-20

The Body and Blood of Christ

Leader: On Corpus Christi Sunday, Jesus gives the gift of himself in the bread and wine.

Narrator: At Passover time, the disciples asked Jesus,

First Disciple: Jesus, where should we go to prepare our Passover meal?

Jesus: Go into Jerusalem. You will meet a man carrying a jar of water. Follow him and when he goes into a house, ask for the owner. Say to him, "Our teacher wants to know where the room is where he can share the Passover meal with his disciples." He will take you to a room that is all ready. You can prepare the meal there.

Narrator: The two disciples went to Jerusalem and found everything as Jesus told them.

Second Disciple: It is just like Jesus said.

First Disciple: We should get busy and prepare the meal. The others will be here shortly.

Narrator: After they arrived the disciples sat at the table. Jesus took bread in his hands, broke it, and said,

Jesus: Take it, this is my body.

Narrator: Then Jesus took a cup of wine, thanked God for it, and shared it with the disciples. He said,

Jesus: This is my blood, the blood of the new promise. This blood is given up for many. I will not drink any more wine until I am with God.

Narrator: They all sang songs of praise to God and walked together to the Mount of Olives.

Where have you heard Jesus' words, "This is my body, this is my blood," before?

Who did Jesus give up his life for?

Sunday After Trinity Sunday   Year B   Mark 14:12-16; 22-26

We Have Found the Messiah

Leader: In today's gospel, Jesus begins to choose his disciples. Two of his first disciples were friends of John the Baptist. One of these disciples was Andrew, the brother of Simon.

Narrator: As John the Baptist stood with two of his disciples, Jesus walked by. John stared hard at him, then said,

John the Baptist: Behold, there is the Lamb of God.

Narrator: Andrew and the other disciple followed Jesus.

Jesus: What are you looking for?

Andrew: Teacher, where are you staying?

Jesus: Come with me and I'll show you.

Narrator: Andrew and the other disciple went with Jesus. Then the next morning Andrew went and found his brother Simon Peter. To Simon, Andrew said,

Andrew: We have found the Messiah, the Anointed One.

Simon: Take me to meet him.

Narrator: Andrew and Simon went to see Jesus. Like before, Jesus stared hard at Simon.

Andrew: Jesus, this is my brother, Simon.

Jesus: You are Simon, the son of John. I will call you Peter.

Why did John call Jesus the Lamb of God?

Why do you think Jesus stared hard upon meeting these disciples?

Second Sunday in Ordinary Time   Year B   John 1:35-42

Even the Evil Spirits Obey Him

Leader: Sometimes even Jesus' closest disciples didn't know who he was or what his mission was. Yet, Satan, the evil one, who often lived inside of people who Jesus met always recognized Jesus as God's Son.

Narrator: In Capernaum, Jesus went into the synagogue to teach. The people were very interested in what he said, because he taught with authority. Suddenly a possessed man came before him.

Man with Evil Spirit: Jesus from Nazareth! What do you want from us? Have you come to destroy us? I know who you are! You are God's Holy One.

Jesus (*to the man with the evil spirit*): **Be quiet and come out of that man!**

Narrator: The evil spirit shook the man, the man let out a loud shriek, and the evil spirit left him. The people were astonished.

First Person: What does this mean?

Second Person: It must be some kind of new, powerful teaching.

Third Person: Even the evil spirits obey him.

Fourth Person: I'm going to go tell everyone about him.

Why do you think all the people with evil spirits knew Jesus?

Why did the evil spirit obey Jesus?

Fourth Sunday in Ordinary Time   Year B   Mark 1:21-28

Healing the Sick

Leader: Throughout his ministry Jesus cured many people who suffered from diseases of one kind or another.

Narrator: After leaving the synagogue, Jesus went with James and John straight to the house of Simon and Andrew.

Andrew: Jesus, come quickly. Simon needs you.

Simon: My mother-in-law is ill.

Jesus: I will help her.

Narrator: Jesus found Simon's mother-in-law in bed with a fever. Jesus went to her, took her by the hand, and helped her up.

Woman: I feel so much better. The fever is gone! Let me fix you dinner.

Narrator: That night, after sunset, the disciples brought many ill people from the town to Simon and Andrew's house. In fact, most of the town crowded around the door. Jesus told them,

Jesus: I will help everyone and make you better.

Narrator: Jesus cured all the sick people there before retiring for the night. Long before it was morning, Jesus went off to a lonely place so that he could pray. Simon and the others went to find him.

Simon: Everyone is looking for you!

John: They have heard how you healed the sick.

Jesus: It is time to go to other towns nearby and tell the good news to those people. That is why I have come.

What did Simon's mother-in-law do after Jesus healed her?

How do you think the people's faith played a part in their being healed?

Fifth Sunday in Ordinary Time   Year B   Mark 1:29-39

Jesus Cures a Leper

Leader: Leprosy is an extremely contagious disease of the skin that causes severe deformation. In Jesus' time lepers were forbidden from coming near healthy people. Yet, in today's gospel, a leper approaches Jesus.

Narrator: The leper pleaded on his knees before Jesus, saying:

Leper: You have the power to make me well. You only have to will it.

Jesus: I do want you to be better. You are healed.

Narrator: At once the man was healed.

Jesus: Do not tell anyone about this. Just go and show yourself to the priest and take a gift of thanksgiving to him. Then everyone will know that you are healed.

Leper: Thank you so much! I am made new! I must tell everyone that you healed me!

Narrator: The leper told everyone that Jesus had healed the leprosy. Because of this Jesus could no longer go directly into town. People came from all over to have Jesus heal them.

Why do you think Jesus told the man not to tell how he was healed?

Why do you think the man ignored Jesus' wishes?

Sixth Sunday in Ordinary Time   Year B   Mark 1:40-45

Your Sins Are Forgiven

Leader: Today's gospel reveals not only Jesus' power to heal illness, but his authority to forgive sins.

Narrator: While Jesus was at home in Capernaum and the room was so crowded that people were spilling out the door, some people carried a crippled person through the streets.

First Person: Let us through! This man is ill!

Second Person: He needs to see Jesus! Jesus can cure him!

Crippled Person: You cannot get me through this crowd. I will not get to see Jesus.

First Person: Come on. I have an idea! We can lower him through the roof!

Second Person: We will have to cut a hole through the roof!

Narrator: After a hole was cut in the roof, the crippled person was lowered down to where Jesus was. Then Jesus addressed the person.

Jesus: My friend, your sins are forgiven.

Narrator: Some teachers of the law discussed among one another what happened.

First Teacher: Why would Jesus say such a thing?

Second Teacher: He must think he is God.

Third Teacher: Yes! Only God can forgive sins.

Jesus: I know what you are thinking. Is it easier for me to tell this man that his sins are forgiven or to tell him to pick up his mat and go home? I will show you that the Son of Man has the right to forgive sins on earth.

Narrator: Then to the man Jesus said,

Jesus: Get up! Pick up your mat and go home.

Narrator: Joyously, the man picked up his mat and walked out in front of everyone.

All: We have never seen anything like it!

Why were the teachers so mad at Jesus?

What is so hard about forgiving someone?

Seventh Sunday in Ordinary Time   Year B   Mark 2:1-12

New Wine, Old Wineskins

Leader: Fasting is a sign of penance. Fasting occasionally from food and drink was a common practice among Jews in Jesus' time. For example, John the Baptist and his followers may have lived in the desert and eaten grasshoppers as part of their diet. Yet, a person would never fast at a wedding as a wedding is a time of celebration. This is the message of today's gospel. Jesus, the bridegroom, is still with them.

First Man: Why don't your disciples ever fast?

Second Man: The disciples of John the Baptist fast.

Third Man: The disciples of the Pharisees fast twice a week.

Fourth Man: So why don't your disciples fast?

Jesus: No one fasts at the wedding feast. The friends of the bridegroom do not fast while he is with them. The time will come when he will be taken from them. Then they will not eat. No one patches old clothes by putting new cloth on them. The new cloth would pull away and make the hole larger. Also, no one puts new wine into old wine skins. The new wine would swell and burst the skins. New wine must be put in new skins.

Why did people think that Jesus and his disciples should fast?

How would you act if Jesus came to share a meal at your home?

Eighth Sunday in Ordinary Time   Year B   Mark 2:18-22

The Lord of the Sabbath

Leader: Saturday is the Sabbath, or holy day, for Jews. According to Jewish law, work of any kind is forbidden on the Sabbath. When Jesus' disciples were found disobeying this law his enemies wondered why.

Narrator: Jesus and his disciples were walking through a field. Some of the disciples picked a few grains from the stalks and ate the wheat. The Pharisees who observed this said to Jesus,

First Pharisee: Why are your disciples picking grain on the Sabbath?

Second Pharisee: Everyone knows it is wrong to work on the Sabbath!

Jesus: Haven't you read in holy scripture what David did when he and his followers were hungry? They entered the house of God and ate the sacred loaves of bread that only priests are allowed to eat. People were not made for the good of the Sabbath. The Sabbath was made for the good of people. The Son of Man is Lord even of the Sabbath.

Narrator: Jesus and his disciples then entered a meeting place. Jesus saw a man with a crippled hand and said to him,

Jesus: Stand up so everyone can see you.

Narrator: The man stood up. Then Jesus turned again to the Pharisees.

Jesus: On the Sabbath should we do good deeds or evil deeds? Should we save someone's life or destroy it?

Narrator: No one answered Jesus, so Jesus said to the crippled man,

Jesus: Stretch out your hand.

Crippled Man: My hand is healed! It is not shriveled up anymore! Thank you, Jesus.

Narrator: The Pharisees went outside of the synagogue.

First Pharisee: Did you see that? He healed on the Sabbath.

Second Pharisee: This cannot be allowed. We must do away with this Jesus.

Is it ever right to break a law? When?

What did Jesus mean, "The Son of Man is Lord even of the Sabbath"?

Ninth Sunday in Ordinary Time   Year B   Mark 2:23–3:6

Who Are My Mother and My Brothers?

Leader: In the greatest absurdity and misunderstanding of all, some of Jesus' enemies even went so far as to say that he performed his miracles in Satan's name and that he was possessed by Satan.

Narrator: Jesus returned again to his hometown of Nazareth. A relative of Jesus approached and said,

Relative of Jesus: We have come to take Jesus home. He has been acting strange lately.

Narrator: Some scribes added,

First Scribe: He is possessed by Satan.

Second Scribe: He uses Satan's power to expel demons.

Jesus: Come here. I want to talk to everyone. How can Satan expel himself? That would be like a nation fighting a war against itself. If a family fights against itself, it will not last very long. So, if Satan were to fight himself, he wouldn't last very long either. No one can break into the house and steal from a strong man unless he first ties up that man. Then he can steal everything. Satan is that strong man. I am in the process of tying him up for good.

Narrator: Jesus continued teaching,

Jesus: I promise you that any sin that you commit can be forgiven, no matter how terrible it is. But if you speak against the Holy Spirit, you can never be forgiven. You will hold this sin forever.

First Disciple: Jesus, why do you tell us all of this?

Jesus: Because they are saying I have an evil spirit, and that is speaking against the spirit that I do have, which is the Holy Spirit.

Narrator: A messenger interrupted him with a message from outside the house.

Messenger: Jesus, your mother and brothers are here to see you.

Jesus *(looks around)***:** Who are my mother and my brothers? Everyone here is my mother and brother. Anyone who obeys God is my mother and my brother and my sister.

How did Jesus explain that it was ridiculous for him to be called Satan?

According to Jesus, who are his mother and brother and sister?

Tenth Sunday in Ordinary Time   Year B   Mark 3:20-35

A Mustard Seed

Leader: Have you ever planted a seed and waited for it to sprout? Jesus tells us the kingdom of God is like planting a seed. It takes patience and care but eventually, everything we wait for will be ours.

Narrator: Jesus addressed the crowds in these words:

Jesus: God's kingdom is like a farmer planting seeds. He plants his seeds during the day, and sleeps at night. Night and day the seeds sprout and grow. The farmer says,

Farmer: Look, the seeds I have planted are starting to sprout. I don't know how that happens.

Jesus: It is the ground that causes the seeds to grow; first the shoot, then the ear, then the full grain in the ear.

Farmer: When this crop is ready, I will cut it. Then I can use it for my family or sell it.

Narrator: Someone in the crowd wondered,

Person in Crowd: What is God's kingdom like?

Jesus: Let me tell you a story to explain it. It is like a mustard seed planted in the ground. It is the smallest seed, but when it sprouts and grows, it is larger than the other plants in the garden. It will grow large enough for birds to nest in the branches.

Narrator: After sharing this parable, Jesus and his disciples left the crowd to be alone.

First Disciple: Jesus, why do you always talk to the people using stories?

Jesus: What I have to tell them is very hard. The stories help them to understand.

Second Disciple: When we're by ourselves, will you tell us exactly what those stories mean?

Jesus: Yes. It is very important for you to understand everything.

Who helps your faith to grow?

What do you want to know about God's kingdom?

Eleventh Sunday in Ordinary Time   Year B   Mark 4:26-34

The Calming of the Storm

Leader: We know that Jesus is God and has God's power. In today's gospel, he shows that even the wind and the sea obey him.

Narrator: Jesus was being pressed by the crowds along the lake. He said,

Jesus: I am tired. Let's leave this crowd and take the boat to the other side of the lake.

Narrator: Once on the boat with his disciples, Jesus fell asleep. Then it began to blow a gale and waves were crashing hard against the boat.

First Disciple: A storm is coming. The wind is blowing hard.

Second Disciple: The waves are too big. The water is coming into the boat!

Third Disciple: Start bailing out the water! I'm afraid we're going to sink!

Fourth Disciple: Wake up Jesus! He'll know what to do!

Fifth Disciple: Wake up, Jesus!

Sixth Disciple: The storm is getting bad!

Seventh Disciple: We're afraid the boat will sink.

Eighth Disciple: Teacher, don't you care that we're about to drown?

Narrator: Jesus rubbed his eyes and looked out to the sea. Then he commanded,

Jesus: Wind! Be quiet! Waves! Be still!

Ninth disciple: Look. The storm is quieting down.

Jesus: Why were you all so afraid? Where is your faith?

Tenth Disciple: I can't believe what I just saw!

Eleventh Disciple: He told the wind and the waves to be calm, and they obeyed him.

Twelfth Disciple: Who do you think he is that he has power over the wind and the sea?

Was it normal for the disciples to be afraid?

How would you react if you saw someone quiet the wind and the sea?

Twelfth Sunday in Ordinary Time   Year B   Mark 4:35-41

Your Faith Has Cured You

Leader: Crowds of sick people always came to Jesus because they had heard that he could cure anyone. In today's gospel, we hear that sometimes a healing was asked for, other times it was granted on faith alone.

Narrator: When Jesus crossed the lake, a large crowd gathered around him. One of the synagogue officials, Jairus, approached Jesus and fell to his knees.

Jairus: My little girl is very sick. If you would just come and touch her, I know she would get better.

Narrator: Jesus called only for Peter, John, and James to go to the man's house. Still, a large crowd pressed against him. In the crowd was an old woman with a hemorrhage who had heard about Jesus. Spotting him, she said,

Old Woman (reaching out to touch Jesus): If I just touch his clothing, I know he can make me better.

Jesus (trying to find the person who touched him): **Who touched me?**

Disciple: There are so many people here. Anyone could have touched you.

Old Woman (kneeling): I have been sick for a long time. I knew that you could make me well with just your touch.

Jesus: Your faith has cured you. You will feel no more pain from this sickness.

Narrator: While he was still speaking some people from Jairus's house came out to meet him and tell him that his daughter had died.

Jesus: Why is everyone crying and carrying on like this? The little girl is not dead! She is just sleeping. Jairus, you and your wife come with me and James, John, and Peter.

Narrator: Near the bedside of the girl Jesus said,

Jesus: Little girl, get up!

Little Girl (rises and starts walking around): I am well now.

Jesus: Don't tell anyone what you have seen here today. Give her some food to eat now. She is cured.

How was the old woman cured of her sickness?

Why do you think Jesus told the girl's parents not to tell anyone what he had done?

Thirteenth Sunday in Ordinary Time   Year B   Mark 5:21-43

Jesus Returns Home

Leader: Jesus wanted to teach the people of his hometown, Nazareth. When he went there, the people only wanted to remember the Jesus they knew as a child. They didn't possibly think he could teach them anything new.

Narrator: Jesus and his disciples went to Jesus' hometown. With the coming of the Sabbath, Jesus wanted to teach the people in the synagogue. The people were astonished by his words.

First Person: How did he learn so much about the scriptures?

Second Person: How did he get his wisdom?

Third Person: Where did he learn to work miracles?

Fourth Person: Isn't his father the carpenter, Joseph? All of his relatives live nearby.

Fifth Person: I didn't come to the synagogue to be taught by a carpenter's son.

Jesus: I can work no miracles here. You people have no faith. People who don't even know me are sure of who I am, but you from my hometown do not believe.

Sixth Person: I have heard he touched some of the sick people and cured them of their sickness.

Seventh Person: I would have to see it myself to believe it.

Jesus: I cannot stay here where people have no faith. I will go to other towns nearby instead to do my teaching.

Why didn't the people of Nazareth believe in Jesus or his teachings?

What does Jesus need in order to work miracles?

Fourteenth Sunday in Ordinary Time   Year B   Mark 6:1-6

Instructions to the Apostles

Leader: In today's gospel, Jesus calls the apostles together and gives them their mission.

Narrator: After summoning the apostles, Jesus said,

Jesus: It is time for you twelve to go out and tell people about what you have seen. I want you to go to the towns nearby. Go in groups of two. I will give you power to cast out evil spirits.

First Apostle: Lord, we will need supplies and donkeys to carry our things.

Jesus: I want you to travel with only a walking stick. Take no money, no food, no extra clothes. Wear sandals on your feet. When you enter a town, stay with the family that welcomes you. If any place does not welcome you or listen to what you have to say, leave that place and reject the people. As you walk away, shake the dust from your feet as a sign to them.

Second Apostle: We will do as you say, Jesus.

Third Apostle: We will tell everyone to live like God wants them to.

Narrator: The apostles set off to preach repentance and they cast out many evil spirits and cured many sick people.

Where did the apostles get the power to cure the sick?

Why do you think Jesus wanted the apostles to travel with so few things?

Fifteenth Sunday in Ordinary Time   Year B   Mark 6:7-13

Like Sheep Without a Shepherd

Leader: When Jesus met the crowds, he taught them, for they were like sheep without a shepherd.

Narrator: The apostles returned to Jesus and told him all they had done and taught.

First Apostle: We did what you told us to do. We expelled many demons!

Second Apostle: We cured many sick people.

Third Apostle: We told many about you!

Jesus: The crowds are starting to follow us here. Let's go off by ourselves for a while and rest.

Fourth Apostle: We could take the boat and go to a place that's not crowded.

Narrator: And that's what they did. Those in the crowd saw them leaving. One of them shouted,

Person in Crowd: Look! Let's follow them. We have heard that they can cure the sick people and get rid of evil spirits.

Narrator: All the people rushed by foot around the shoreline to meet Jesus on the other side. They beat him there.

Fifth Apostle: Look at the large crowd! All those people have beat us here.

Sixth Apostle: We won't be able to rest here, either.

Jesus: Those poor, poor people. They are like sheep without a shepherd. I have much to teach them, if they will listen to me.

Why did the people rush to the other side of the lake?

What did Jesus mean, "They are like sheep without a shepherd"?

Sixteenth Sunday in Ordinary Time   Year B   Mark 6:30-34

I Am the Bread of Life

Leader: Whoever comes to Jesus will never be hungry. Whoever believes in him will never thirst.

Narrator: After Jesus fed five thousand people with only five loaves and two fish, he left the crowd for Capernaum. The people went searching for him.

First Person: Where did Jesus go? We were here eating bread with him and now he's gone.

Second Person: Let's go to the other side of the lake. Maybe that's where he went.

Narrator: The people took boats to get to the other side of the lake. That's where they found him.

Third Person (*finding Jesus*)**:** Look, there he is! Teacher, when did you come here?

Jesus: I know that you are looking for me only because I gave you bread to eat. You should not be working for food that will spoil. You should work for food that will give you life that will last forever. You can get this food from the Son of Man, because he was sent by God the Father.

Fourth Person: What does the Father want us to do?

Jesus: You must have faith in the one he sent.

Fifth Person: If we are to believe that you were sent by God, you must work a miracle. When our ancestors were in the desert with Moses, they received manna to eat.

Jesus: It was not Moses who gave them the bread from heaven. It is my Father who gives you the real heavenly bread. God's bread comes down from heaven and gives life to the world.

Sixth Person: Give us that bread to eat. That's the bread we want.

Jesus: I am the bread of life. No one who comes to me will ever be hungry. No one who believes in me will ever thirst again.

Why did Jesus say the crowd followed him?

How do Jesus' words "I am the bread of life" help you to understand eucharist?

Eighteenth Sunday in Ordinary Time   Year B   John 6:24-35

I Will Raise You Up on the Last Day

Leader: Jesus is the living bread that came down from heaven. We need Jesus so we can be closer to God the Father.

Jesus: I am the bread that has come down from heaven.

First Person: I know his mother and father. He is Jesus, son of Joseph.

Second Person: Right. How can he claim to have come from heaven? We know he is from Nazareth.

Jesus: Stop grumbling. No one can come to me, unless the Father in heaven wants them to. If you do come to me, I will raise you up on the last day. The prophets say,

Voice of the Prophet: God will teach them all.

Jesus: Everyone who learns from the Father will come to me. No one has seen the Father except the one who is from God. This is certain: anyone who believes in me will have eternal life. I am the bread that gives life. Your ancestors ate bread in the desert and they later died. I am the bread from heaven that has come down. Anyone who eats this bread will have life forever. My body is the bread that I give to the world.

Why did some people complain about Jesus?

What does Jesus promise to those who come to him?

Nineteenth Sunday in Ordinary Time   Year B   John 6:41-51

Eat My Body, Drink My Blood

Leader: Jesus tells the crowds, "My flesh is real food and my blood is real drink."

Jesus: I am the bread from heaven. Anyone who eats this bread will live forever. My body is the bread that I give to the world.

First Person: How can he give us his flesh to eat?

Second Person: His body is not bread.

Third Person: We can't believe what he says.

Jesus: This you must know. Unless you eat the body of the Son of Man and drink his blood, you will have no life in you. If you do eat my body and drink my blood, you will have everlasting life and I will raise you up on the last day. My flesh is the true food and my blood is the true drink. If you eat my flesh and drink my blood we will be one with another. The Father sent me and I have life because of Him. Now, you have life because of me. The bread your ancestors ate in the desert did not give them everlasting life. But anyone who eats this bread will live forever.

Why do you think some people had so much trouble believing Jesus is the bread from heaven?

What does Jesus say will happen when we eat his body and drink his blood?

Twentieth Sunday in Ordinary Time   Year B   John 6:51-58

Who Else Could We Follow?

Leader: Jesus' message is difficult to understand. He told the people they must eat his body and drink his blood to have eternal life. Many of his followers left him because of these words. Other disciples stayed because they realized that Jesus had the words of eternal life.

Narrator: After hearing his words "I am the bread" the disciples conversed,

First Follower: How can he say his flesh is bread?

Second Follower: This is too hard to understand.

Third Follower: How can anyone believe this?

Jesus: Does this talk shock you? What if you were to see the Son of Man go up to heaven where he came from? The Spirit is the one who gives life. What I have said came from the Spirit. I have always known that some of you do not have faith in me. That is why I said you cannot come to me unless the Father wants you to.

Narrator: Jesus knew which of the disciples had faith in him and he also knew which one would betray him.

Fourth Follower: I am not listening to this anymore.

Fifth Follower: I cannot follow Jesus. I'm going home.

Narrator: Then Jesus addressed his twelve apostles.

Jesus: Will you leave me too?

Narrator: Peter spoke up for the Twelve.

Peter: Lord, who else could we follow? You're the one who has the words of everlasting life. We believe and are convinced that you are God's Holy One.

What did some of Jesus' followers find hard?

Peter and the Twelve stayed with Jesus because he has the words of eternal life.
Why do you stay with Jesus?

Twenty-First Sunday in Ordinary Time   Year B   John 6:60-69

Follow God's Commandment

Leader: Human traditions are not as important as God's commandments. In today's gospel, Jesus reminds us of this important lesson.

Narrator: The Pharisees and some of the scribes had come from Jerusalem. They talked among themselves.

First Pharisee: Look, Jesus' disciples have not washed their hands before they eat.

Second Pharisee: That is wrong. They must know that everything must be washed carefully— their hands up to the elbow, and the utensils.

Third Pharisee: Jesus, why don't you and your disciples follow the Jewish customs?

Jesus: You are all just show offs. The prophet Isaiah was right when he wrote,

Voice of Isaiah: You praise me with words but you never really think of me. It is worthless for you to worship me when all you do is follow rules made up by humans.

Jesus: You pay more attention to human traditions than God's commandments. Listen to me and understand. The food that you eat does not make you unclean or unfit to worship God. It is the bad words that come out of your mouth that will make you impure. Out of your heart come evil thoughts and bad deeds. Out of your heart comes disrespect for the body, stealing, murder, unfaithfulness in marriage, greed, meanness, deceit, indecency, envy, insults, pride, and foolishness. This is what makes you unfit to worship God.

What is the most important lesson of this gospel?

What are some things that make us unfit to worship God?

Twenty-Second Sunday in Ordinary Time   Year B   Mark 7:1-8, 14-15, 21-23

Ears and Tongue Open

Leader: Jesus' miracles are great. He has given the deaf their hearing and the dumb their speech.

Narrator: Jesus was heading to the Sea of Galilee, right through the Decapolis region. A deaf man with a speech impediment was brought to him.

First Person: Jesus, this man is deaf and can hardly speak. Can you help him?

Jesus: Come with me away from this crowd.

Narrator: Away from the crowds, Jesus put his fingers in the man's ears, then touched his tongue with mud. Then, looking up to heaven, he said,

Jesus: Ears and tongue open!

Deaf Man: I can hear! I can talk clearly! You have cured me! Thank you, Jesus.

Jesus: Do not tell anyone what has happened here.

Second Person: He can do everything, even cure the sick.

Third Person: This man was deaf but now he can hear. He was dumb, but now he can speak.

Fourth Person: Everything Jesus does is good! I'm going to tell everyone!

Why do you think Jesus took the man away from the crowds?

Why did they tell everyone what they had seen anyway?

Twenty-Third Sunday in Ordinary Time   Year B   Mark 7:31-37

Pick Up Your Cross and Follow

Leader: Jesus is the Christ, the Son of Man who will face suffering, rejection, and death.

Narrator: On the way to the villages around Caesarea Philippi, Jesus put this question to his disciples:

Jesus: What do people say I am?

First Disciple: Some say you are John the Baptist.

Second Disciple: Others say you are Elijah.

Third Disciple: Some say you are one of the other prophets.

Jesus: But you, who do you say that I am?

Peter: You are the Messiah.

Jesus: Don't tell anyone that yet. The Son of Man will suffer and be rejected by his people. He will die and rise again three days later.

Peter: Jesus, don't talk like that. You aren't going to die.

Jesus: You are Satan! Get away from me! You are not thinking like God.

Narrator: Then Jesus spoke to the crowd and his disciples.

Jesus: If you want to be with me you must forget about yourself. You must pick up your cross and follow my footsteps. If you want to save your life, you will destroy it. You will only save your life if you give up your life for me and the good news.

Why did Peter and Jesus argue?

What does it mean to "pick up your cross" and follow Jesus?

Twenty-Fourth Sunday in Ordinary Time   Year B   Mark 8:27-35

If You Want to Be First . . .

Leader: In today's gospel, though Jesus is about to be handed over and put to death, his disciples argue among them about which one is the greatest.

Jesus: Come with me down the mountain to Galilee. Don't tell anyone where we are going. I need to be alone with you. The time is coming. The Son of Man will be given up to the men who will kill him. Three days after his death he will rise again.

Narrator: While they were walking the disciples talked to each other out of earshot of Jesus.

First Disciple: What does that mean? I don't understand him.

Second Disciple: I'm not sure but I don't want to ask him what he means.

Third Disciple: I could ask him. I'm his favorite disciple.

Fourth Disciple: I don't know about that. I am the one who is always with him.

Fifth Disciple: But I do whatever Jesus tells me to do. I am the one Jesus depends on the most.

Sixth Disciple: Jesus talks to me all the time. I must be his favorite.

Narrator: After Jesus and his disciples entered the house in Galilee, he asked them,

Jesus: What were all of you talking about on the way home?

Narrator: No one answered. They didn't want to tell Jesus that they had been arguing about which one of them was the greatest.

Jesus: If any of you want to be first, you must serve others. To be first, you must be last. Little child, come here.

Narrator: Jesus then placed a small child before them and said,

Jesus: Whoever welcomes a child in my name because of me, welcomes me. And whoever welcomes me, welcomes the one who sent me.

What are we to do if we want to be "first" in Jesus' eyes?

What are ways you can serve others?

Twenty-Fifth Sunday in Ordinary Time   Year B   Mark 9:30-37

Anyone Not Against Us Is For Us

Leader: A message of today's gospel is that anyone who is not against Jesus can actually be counted as for Jesus.

Narrator: The apostle John reported this incident to Jesus:

John: Teacher, we saw a man who was using your name to cast out evil spirits. We didn't know him, so we told him to stop.

Jesus: Don't stop him. Anyone who uses my name to perform a miracle can't say anything bad about me.

First Disciple: I never thought of it like that.

Jesus: Anyone who is not against us is for us. Anyone who even gives you a cup of water because you know me will receive his reward.

Second Disciple: Jesus says that God will reward anyone who is kind to one of his followers.

Jesus: But if anyone leads astray a believer, it would be better if that person were to be thrown into the sea with a rock around his neck.

Third Disciple: No one could lead me astray no matter how hard they tried.

Jesus: If it is your hand that causes you to sin, cut it off. It is better for you to have no hands than to enter hell with both hands. If your foot causes you to sin, cut it off. It is better for you to be crippled in this life than to enter hell with both feet. If it is your eye that causes you to sin, pluck it out. It is better to enter the kingdom of God blind than it is to be thrown into the fires with both eyes. For in hell, the worm never dies and the fires never go out.

How can other people tell that you are a follower of Jesus?

What does Jesus mean when he says, "It is better to enter the kingdom of God blind than to be thrown into hell with both eyes"?

Twenty-Sixth Sunday in Ordinary Time   Year B   Mark 9:38-43, 45, 47-48

Let the Children Come to Me

Leader: In the gospel today, Jesus speaks about marriage, saying that what God has joined together must not be divided. He also tells us that we must be like little children—full of faith—to enter the kingdom of heaven.

Narrator: Some Pharisees approached Jesus and tried to test him.

First Pharisee: Tell us, Jesus, is it right for a man to divorce his wife?

Jesus: What did Moses say?

Second Pharisee: Moses permitted a man to divorce his wife.

Jesus: That is because you are so heartless. God created us as men and women. A man will leave his mother and father, marry a woman, and the two will be as one. They are no longer two people but one. No one should separate what God has joined.

Narrator: Once inside the house, the disciples continued to question Jesus.

First Disciple: Jesus, do you really mean to go against Moses and say that a man cannot divorce his wife?

Jesus: Whoever divorces his wife and marries another is unfaithful. A woman who divorces her husband and marries another is unfaithful to her husband.

Narrator: People were bringing children to Jesus for him to touch.

Second Disciple: Tell them to go away. We are too busy for children.

Jesus: Let the children come to me. I want to see them. It is to children like these that the kingdom of God belongs. You cannot enter the kingdom of God unless you accept it like a child.

Narrator: Jesus blessed the children by placing his hands on them.

Why did Jesus say that it is better that a husband and wife should not divorce?

What do you think it means to accept the kingdom of God like a little child?

Twenty-Seventh Sunday in Ordinary Time   Year B   Mark 10:2-16

Who Can Be Saved?

Leader: Today's gospel tells us the importance of following the commandments of God and doing what we can to help the poor.

Narrator: Jesus was setting out for a journey when a man ran up to him, knelt before him, and asked this question.

Rich Person: Good teacher, please tell me. What can I do to have eternal life?

Jesus: Why do you call me good? No one is good except God. To have eternal life, you must follow the commandments. You know them: You shall not kill. You shall not commit adultery. You shall not steal. You shall not lie. You shall not cheat anyone. You shall honor your mother and father.

Rich Person: Teacher, I have obeyed all these commandments all of my life.

Jesus: There is one more thing you must do. Go and sell what you have and give the money to the poor. You will receive your reward in heaven. Then you can come and follow me.

Rich Person: But I am a very rich man! I have so many things and I don't want to sell everything.

Jesus: It is very hard for the rich to enter heaven. It is easier for a camel to go through the eye of a needle than it is for a rich man to enter heaven.

First Disciple: You can't mean that!

Second Disciple: Then who can be saved?

Jesus: For humans, it is impossible to save themselves, but it is not impossible for God. Everything is possible with God.

Third Disciple: What about us? We gave up everything to be with you.

Jesus: I promise you, anyone who has given up home, brothers or sisters, mother or father, children or property for me or for the gospel will receive their reward. He will receive a hundred times as many homes, brothers and sisters, mothers and fathers, children and property. But that person will also have to suffer in my name as well. In the end, he will be given eternal life.

What did the rich man find hard to do?

What will you do so that you can go to heaven?

Twenty-Eighth Sunday in Ordinary Time   Year B   Mark 10:17-30

You Must Be a Servant

Leader: In the gospel today, Jesus tells us that he did not come to be an earthly king. Rather, he has come to serve and give his life for others.

Narrator: James and John, the sons of Zebedee, approached Jesus. James began. He said,

James: Jesus, we have a favor to ask you.

Jesus: Yes, what is it?

John: When you come into your glory, we would like to sit at your right side and at your left side.

Jesus: You don't know what you are asking. Can you drink from the cup of pain that I am to drink from? Are you willing to be baptized as I must be baptized? Are you willing to go through everything that will soon happen to me?

James: Yes, of course we are.

John: We are ready to follow you anywhere.

Jesus: Then you *will* drink from the cup that I must drink from and you will be baptized as I must be baptized. But as for sitting at my right or my left, that is not mine to give. That is up to the Father. He will decide that.

First Disciple: Why are you asking such favors of Jesus?

Second Disciple: We all would like to sit at his right or his left.

Jesus: Everyone come here. I have something to say. You know how great leaders and kings like to have power over everyone and order them around. It cannot be like that with you. If you are to be great, you must serve other people. If you want to be first, you must be a servant. The Son of Man did not come to be served but to serve other people, and to give his life to rescue others.

Why were the other disciples angry with James and John?

Why did Jesus come to earth?

Twenty-Ninth Sunday in Ordinary Time   Year B   Mark 10:35-45

Healing of Blind Bartimaeus

Leader: In the gospel today, a blind man is cured. Jesus tells him it was his own faith that restored his sight.

Narrator: As Jesus left Jericho with his disciples and a large crowd, Bartimaeus, a blind beggar, was sitting at the side of the road. He heard it was Jesus and began to shout,

Bartimaeus: Jesus, Son of David, have pity on me. Please help me!

First Person: Be quiet! We are trying to hear what Jesus is saying.

Bartimaeus *(shouting louder)*: Son of David, have pity on me.

Second Person: Get out of the way and stop shouting.

Narrator: Jesus stopped and said,

Jesus: Call the blind man over here.

Third Person: Jesus wants to see you. Go over to him.

Fourth Person: Don't be afraid. He is calling for you.

Narrator: Bartimaeus threw off his cloak and stood in front of Jesus.

Jesus: What do you want me to do for you?

Bartimaeus: Teacher, I want to see.

Jesus: Go on your way. Your faith has healed you.

Bartimaeus: I can see! I can see! I will follow you now, Jesus.

How did Bartimaeus feel when Jesus called him? How would you feel?

How was Bartimaeus cured of his blindness?

Thirtieth Sunday in Ordinary Time   Year B   Mark 10:46-52

Love Your Neighbor as Yourself

Leader: In the gospel today, Jesus tells us that the first commandment—to love God—is the same as the second, to love one's neighbor as yourself.

Narrator: One of the scribes came up to Jesus and posed this question:

Scribe: Which is the most important of all the commandments?

Jesus: The most important commandment is this: there is only one Lord and God. You must love him with all your heart, soul, mind, and strength. The second most important commandment is like it: love your neighbor as you love yourself. There is no greater commandment than these.

Scribe: Very good, teacher. You are right to say these are the most important commandments. It is most important to love God and then, second, to love your neighbor. These are more important than to offer sacrifices and burnt offerings to God.

Narrator: Seeing how wisely the scribe had spoken, Jesus said,

Jesus: You are very close to the reign of God.

Narrator: No one dared to ask Jesus any more questions.

How can you show your love for God?

How can you show your love for your neighbor?

Thirty-First Sunday in Ordinary Time   Year B   Mark 12:28-34

The Poor Widow

Leader: Jesus tells us not to show off and brag about the good things we do. We should do good deeds without expecting any reward. Our reward will come in heaven.

Narrator: In teaching the people, Jesus said,

Jesus: Don't be like the scribes. They like to wear their fancy robes so everyone knows who they are. They like to think they are important. They sit in the front row at the banquets and at synagogues. They say long prayers just to show off. They pretend to be holy but they cheat widows out of their homes. These kinds of people will be punished hardest of all.

First Disciple: Jesus, do you see all the people offering money to the Temple?

Jesus: Yes, I see. The rich people are making sure that everyone sees them giving a lot of money. Look over there at that old woman giving her offering.

Old Woman: It is not much, only two coins, but it is all that I have.

Jesus: This woman has given more than anyone else. The rich gave money that they didn't need. This woman gave all that she has to live on.

How did the scribes show off?

Why did Jesus say the poor widow put in more than anyone else?

Thirty-Second Sunday in Ordinary Time   Year B   Mark 12:38-44

No One Knows the Day or the Hour

Leader: In today's gospel Jesus tells his disciples about the time when he will return in glory.

Jesus: There will be a time of suffering, with false messiahs and false prophets.

First Disciple: When will you come back, Jesus?

Jesus: After that time, the sun and moon will be dark and the stars will fall out of the sky. It is then that the Son of Man will come from the clouds in glory. He will send his angels to gather his chosen people from all over the earth.

Second Disciple: I hope the angels come for me.

Third Disciple: When will we know that time is near?

Jesus: Think of a fig tree. When the tree starts to get its leaves, you know summer is near. When you see the things happening that I have said, you will know that the time is almost here for the Son of Man to come. I tell you that some of the people from this generation will still be alive when all this happens. The heavens and earth will not last forever, but my words will.

Fourth Disciple: Won't you tell us an exact date for these things to happen?

Jesus: No one knows exactly when this time will come. Not the angels, not even the Son of Man. Only the Father knows.

What is the message of the fig tree?

Why do we not know exactly when Jesus will return?

Thirty-Third Sunday in Ordinary Time   Year B   Mark 13:24-32

Jesus Is King

Leader: We celebrate the feast of Christ the King, though Jesus is not a typical earthly king like we may be used to hearing about.

Narrator: After Jesus was arrested, Pontius Pilate, the Roman governor, questioned him.

Pilate: Are you the king of the Jews?

Jesus: Are you asking this for yourself or has someone else been telling you about me?

Pilate: I am not a Jew! It was your own people and the chief priests that brought you to me. What have you done?

Jesus: My kingdom is not of this world. If it were of this world, my followers would have fought to keep me from being turned over to you. No, my kingdom is not of this world.

Pilate: So! You are a king!

Jesus: You are the one who says I am a king. The reason I was born was to tell about the truth. Anyone who knows about the truth knows my voice.

Is Jesus a king?

Where is Jesus' kingdom?

Last Sunday in Ordinary Time   Year B   John 18:33-37

Sunday Gospels

(with Christmas and New Year's Gospels)

Year C

Keep Watch

Leader: Advent is a time of waiting, a time of preparation. We are preparing our hearts and our souls for our Savior. In the gospel today, Jesus tells his disciples that there will be many signs before he comes again.

Jesus: Before the Son of Man comes in glory, there will be many signs.

First Disciple: What kind of signs?

Jesus: The sun, the moon, and the stars will do strange things.

Second Disciple: That will frighten everyone to see strange things in the sky.

Jesus: The seas and the tides will frighten the people and they won't know what to do. Some will faint in fear. Every power in the sky will be shaken.

Third Disciple: I can't imagine living through all of that.

Jesus: After that time, the Son of Man will come in the clouds in glory. When this happens, stand up straight and be brave because you will be free.

Fourth Disciple: What should we do now to prepare for this?

Jesus: Don't spend all your time eating and drinking too much. Don't worry about your life. You must be careful or the last day will spring on you like a trap.

Fifth Disciple: When will this happen?

Jesus: The last day will come as a surprise to everyone on earth. Pray that only good will happen to you. Pray that the Son of Man will be pleased with you.

What do you think the world will be like right before Jesus comes again?

What should we pray for?

First Sunday in Advent   Year C   Luke 21:25-28, 34-36

Turn Away From Sin

Leader: In the gospel today, John the Baptist tells us to run away from sin. This was his God-appointed mission as he readied the Jews of Palestine for the coming of Christ.

First Narrator: The Emperor Tiberius was the ruler of that part of the world for fifteen years. Pontius Pilate was the governor of Judea, and Herod ruled Galilee. Philip, Herod's brother, ruled Iturea and Trachonitis. Lysanias ruled Abilene. Annas and Caiaphas were the Jewish high priests.

Second Narrator: At that time, God spoke to John, Zechariah's son, who lived in the desert. He told John it was time to begin his mission, to prepare the way for the Messiah.

John the Baptist: Turn away from sin! Turn back to God! Be baptized and your sins will be forgiven!

Third Narrator: Isaiah the prophet was writing about John the Baptist in these words:

Writings of Isaiah: Someone is shouting in the desert, make the road ready, for the Lord is coming. Make the road straight! Fill in all the valleys and level all the mountains and hills. Straighten the paths and smooth the rough roads! Then everyone will see God's saving power!

What do Isaiah's words mean? How can anyone "fill in valleys" or "level mountains"?

What is one way you can turn back to God?

Second Sunday in Advent   Year C   Luke 3:1-6

Give to One Who Needs It

Leader: In his preaching, John the Baptist tells the crowd to prepare for the Messiah. They have come to him to be baptized and John tells them what it means to lead a good life.

Narrator: A person in the crowd asked John the Baptist,

First Person: What should I do to live a good life?

John the Baptist: Be kind to others. If you have two coats, give one to someone who needs it. If you have food, share it with others also.

Tax Collector: I am a tax collector. I would like to be baptized. What should I do?

John the Baptist: Only charge people the tax that they owe. Do not make them pay any more than that.

Soldier: What about me, a soldier? What should we do?

John the Baptist: Do not bully anyone into paying you money. Do not tell lies about anyone.

Second Person: Do you think John the Baptist is the Messiah?

Third Person: Is he the one we've been waiting for?

John the Baptist: I am baptizing you in water. Someone else is coming who is mightier than I am. I am not worthy to loosen his sandal from his foot. He will baptize you with the Holy Spirit and the fire. He will separate the husks from the wheat. He will store the wheat in the barn and will throw the husks into the fire that never goes out.

Besides baptism, what else must we do to live a good life?

How are you kind to others?

Third Sunday in Advent   Year C   Luke 3:10-18

The Visitation

Leader: In the gospel today, Mary visits Elizabeth. Both women are expecting babies. Elizabeth's son is John the Baptist, and Mary's son is Jesus.

Narrator: Mary traveled to Judea. She went to Zechariah and Elizabeth's house.

Mary: Hello, Elizabeth. I have come a long way to visit you.

Narrator: Elizabeth, filled with the Holy Spirit, says in a loud voice,

Elizabeth: I am so happy to see you! Blessed are you among women and blessed is the fruit of your womb. Why did you, the mother of my Lord, come to see me? The moment I heard your voice I was so happy, and even my baby who has not been born yet moved for joy inside of me. God blessed you because you believed he would keep his promise to you.

Why was Elizabeth happy to see Mary?

In which familiar prayer do you pray Elizabeth's words?

Fourth Sunday in Advent   Year C   Luke 1:39-45

Jesus Is Found in the Temple

Leader: This gospel is the only recorded incident of Jesus' childhood. At twelve years old Jesus has traveled with his family to Jerusalem for the Passover. The gospel begins on their return home to Nazareth.

Narrator: Thinking Jesus was in the caravan of friends and family on the way home, Mary and Joseph did not miss him until they had been outside of Jerusalem for a day. Mary wondered,

Mary: Have you seen Jesus?

Joseph: He's traveling with some of his cousins. He's twelve now and old enough that he doesn't have to stay with us all the time.

Mary: We should try to find him.

Narrator: Mary and Joseph searched for him with all of their friends and acquaintances.

Mary: Joseph, I have looked everywhere. No one has seen Jesus!

Joseph: I have asked everyone. No one has seen Jesus since we left Jerusalem.

Mary: We have to go back to Jerusalem and find him. I hope that he is all right.

Narrator: Mary and Joseph returned to Jerusalem and found Jesus sitting in the midst of the Jewish teachers at the Temple.

First Teacher: I have never heard such wisdom from anyone, let alone a boy his age.

Second Teacher: This Jesus certainly knows the scriptures well.

Mary: Son, why did you do this to us? We have been looking for you for three days. We didn't know where you were and we were so scared that something bad had happened to you.

Jesus: Why did you have to look for me? Didn't you know I would be in my Father's house?

Narrator: His parents didn't understand what he meant. They all went back to Nazareth, and Jesus was obedient to his parents. Mary remembered all that had happened. Jesus grew in wisdom and God's grace was with him.

Why do you think Jesus stayed in Jerusalem when everyone else left?

What did Jesus mean by "Why did you have to look for me?"

Holy Family   Year C   Luke 2:41-52

Lesson of the Fig Tree

Leader: This gospel tells us the importance of being sorry for our sins and looking for ways to repent.

Narrator: Some people arrived and told Jesus some horrifying news about some Galileans.

First Person: Jesus, did you hear about the Galileans? While they were sacrificing some animals Pontius Pilate ordered them to be killed. Then their blood was mixed with the blood of the animals that they were sacrificing.

Jesus: Don't think that they were the worst sinners because they suffered like that. They were not the biggest sinners in Galilee. But you can be sure that you will die like that if you do not change your ways and live a better life. What about the eighteen people who were killed when the tower of Siloam fell on them? Do you think their sins were worse than any other people in Jerusalem? No, they were not. But you will die like that unless you turn back to God. I would like to tell you a story about the owner of a vineyard and a vine dresser. The story goes like this:

Vineyard Owner: This fig tree has no fruit. I have looked for fruit on this tree for three years, and it never has produced any figs. It is just taking up space. I want it cut down.

Vine Dresser: Please, sir, let me take care of it. I will hoe the weeds around it and fertilize it. Maybe with good care, it will produce fruit. If it does not have any figs growing on it in one year, then we will cut it down.

What does the fig tree with no fruit represent?

What does this story mean to you?

Third Sunday of Lent   Year C   Luke 13:1-9

The Prodigal Son

Leader: Today's gospel is the famous parable of the prodigal son. Prodigal means "extravagant" or wasteful. In the story Jesus tells, one son ran off, the other stayed but resented working for his father. The message is the same: Return home. Return to the merciful Father.

Narrator: Jesus was teaching the tax collectors and sinners. A Pharisee noted,

Pharisee: Jesus welcomes sinners and eats with them. We would never do that.

Jesus: Let me tell you this story about a father and his two sons. It goes like this:

Younger Son: Father, I don't want to wait for my inheritance. Give it to me now so I can live my life like I want to.

Father: I will give you your share of my money and I will give your older brother his share. Usually, sons wait for their father to die before they get their inheritance. But if you want it now, I will give it to you.

Younger Son: I am going to live in a different country. I have heard that it is easy there and a lot of fun.

Jesus: The younger son did go to another country, spent all of his money, and then thought to himself:

Younger Son: I don't have any money left. I don't even have enough for food. The farmer's pigs eat better than I do. I would be happy to eat the husks of corn the pigs eat. I'm going back home to my father's house. His servants are treated better than I am in this strange land. I will ask my father to forgive me for leaving. I will tell him that all I would like is to be a servant for him.

Jesus: As the younger son traveled home, his father saw him from a distance.

Father: There is a traveler. It looks like my younger son. It *is* him! I can't believe he has come home! I must go to see him!

Jesus: The father ran down the road, threw his arms around his son, and kissed him.

Younger Son: Father, I don't deserve to be your son. I have sinned, against you and against God.

Father (*to servant*): Quick! Bring new clothes! Bring new shoes! We will have a feast to celebrate! My son was gone and he has come home!

Narrator: The older son noticed all the commotion and said to the servant,

Older Son: What is going on here? What is this party for?

Servant: Your brother is home and your father is so happy. We are having a party, with lots of food.

Older Son: I'm not going to a party for my brother. My father should be mad at him for coming home with nothing.

Narrator: The father found his older son standing alone outside.

Father: Son, please come in to celebrate with us.

Older Son: I have worked hard for you for many years. You have never had a party for me. I never disobeyed you. Now my brother comes home after wasting all of his money, and you throw a big party for him.

Father: Son, you know I love you. You have always been with me, and everything I have is yours. But we must celebrate! Your brother was lost, and he has come home. It's as if he was dead and has come back to life.

Do you think the younger son was afraid to come home? Why or why not?

Why was the older son angry with his father?

How is God the Father like the father in this story?

Fourth Sunday of Lent   Year C   Luke 15:1-3, 11-32

Go and Sin No More

Leader: As we continue our preparation for Easter, we find hope in today's gospel as Jesus forgives a public sinner.

Narrator: Jesus began to teach the people who gathered in the Temple area. The Pharisees brought a woman to the middle of the crowd and spoke to Jesus.

First Pharisee: Jesus, this woman has sinned. She has been unfaithful to her husband. The law says she should be stoned. What do you say?

Narrator: Jesus stooped down and drew in the sand, ignoring them.

Second Pharisee: Jesus. We are talking to you. This woman has sinned. What should we do with her?

Jesus: If you have never sinned, then throw stones at her.

Narrator: Again, Jesus stooped to the ground and wrote in the sand, ignoring those around him.

First Person: What does that mean? Everyone has sinned.

Second Person: He said not to throw a stone unless *we* have never sinned.

Narrator: Everyone left, except the woman and Jesus, who was still writing in the sand. Then Jesus stood up and looked at the woman.

Jesus: Where did everyone go? Isn't there anyone left to punish you?

Woman: No one, sir.

Jesus: Then I will not punish you either. You may go, but do not sin like this anymore.

Why didn't anyone throw stones at the woman?

When was a time someone forgave you?

Fifth Sunday of Lent   Year C   John 8:1-11

Do You Love Me?

Leader: Jesus appeared to his disciples several times after his resurrection. Though the Lord was always with them, they did not always recognize him.

Narrator: On one occasion Jesus showed himself at the Sea of Tiberias where the disciples were going out to fish. They were on the boat several hours without having any luck. About dawn Jesus stood on the shore, but the disciples did not know it was him.

Jesus: Have you caught anything yet?

First Disciple: Nothing. We've been fishing all night and haven't caught a thing.

Jesus: Try fishing on the other side of your boat. Cast your nets over there and you will find something.

Narrator: The disciples did as he said and the net was so full they could not haul it back up. John, the disciple Jesus loved, recognized Jesus and said to Peter,

John: It is the Lord!

Narrator: Peter jumped into the water and swam to Jesus on shore. They were about one hundred yards from land. The other disciples came in their boat, towing the fish behind them. On shore, they found a fire with fish and bread cooking on it.

Jesus: Bring some of the fish you just caught.

Peter: Jesus, the disciples have counted the fish. There are 153, but still the net did not tear.

Jesus: Come and eat your meal. Here is some bread and fish for you.

Narrator: This was the third time that Jesus appeared to his disciples after he had been raised from the dead. After eating the meal, Jesus spoke directly to Peter.

Jesus: Simon Peter, son of John, do you love me more than these others do?

Peter: Yes, Lord, you know I love you.

Jesus: Feed my lambs. Simon Peter, son of John, do you love me?

Peter: Yes, Lord, you know that I love you.

Jesus: Take care of my sheep. Simon, son of John, do you love me?

Peter: Lord, you know everything. You know that I love you.

Jesus: Feed my sheep. Remember this: when you were young you could do what you wanted and go where you wanted. But when you are older, others will tie your hands and take you somewhere you don't want to go.

Narrator: Jesus said this to show what kind of death Peter would have. After this conversation Jesus said,

Jesus: Follow me.

How would you have felt if someone asked you to try fishing again after you didn't catch one fish all night?

Who are the sheep Jesus asks Peter to care for and feed?

Third Sunday of Easter   Year C   John 21:1-19

I Know My Sheep

Leader: A shepherd takes care of his sheep and knows where each sheep is all of the time. A shepherd rescues a sheep that is in trouble. Jesus is the Good Shepherd.

Jesus: My sheep know my voice and they listen to me.

First Disciple: I know when Jesus speaks to me.

Jesus: I know my sheep and my sheep follow me.

Second Disciple: I will follow Jesus wherever he goes.

Jesus: I give my sheep life forever so they will never die. No one can snatch them from me.

Third Disciple: I am safe with Jesus.

Jesus: My Father has given my sheep to me and there is no one who can take them away from my Father, who is greater than all. My Father and I are one.

Who are Jesus' sheep?

How is Jesus the Good Shepherd?

Fourth Sunday of Easter   Year C   John 10:27-30

Love One Another

Leader: Jesus gives us a new commandment, to love one another as he has loved us.

Narrator: When Jesus left the Upper Room, he said,

Jesus: The Son of Man has glory, and the glory of God is in him.

First Disciple: We have seen the glory of God in you, Jesus.

Jesus: If the Son of Man has brought glory to God, God will bring glory to him. This will be happening very soon.

Second Disciple: What will happen soon?

Jesus: My children, I will not be with you much longer.

Third Disciple: Where are you going, Lord? What will you leave to us?

Jesus: I give to you a new commandment: Love one another as I have loved you.

Third Disciple: I do love you and since I have known you I have come to love all people as brothers and sisters.

Jesus: Everyone will know that you are my disciples by your love for each other.

How do you show your love for God?

How do the people who know you know that you are a disciple of Jesus?

Fifth Sunday of Easter   Year C   John 13:31-33, 34-35

I Leave You Peace

Leader: Jesus tells his disciples what is going to happen before it happens so they will not be afraid. He tells them the Holy Spirit will come to help them.

Jesus: Anyone who loves me will obey me.

First Disciple: I love you, Lord, and I will do as you have said.

Jesus: My Father will love you and we will live in you. If anyone does not love me, that person will not obey me. But what you hear me say comes from the Father, not from me.

Second Disciple: We have listened and tried to remember all that you have said.

Jesus: I have told you a great deal while I am with you. The Father will send the Holy Spirit to you when I am gone.

Third Disciple: What will the Holy Spirit do?

Jesus: The Holy Spirit will teach you and will also remind you of what I said when I was with you.

Fourth Disciple: You sound like you are going away. Are you leaving us?

Jesus: My peace is my goodbye gift to you, but it is a different kind of peace than the rest of the world knows. Do not be afraid.

Fifth Disciple: But we do not want you to leave us, Lord.

Jesus: I have told you that I will go away for a while and then I will come back to you. You should be happy that I am going to be with my Father. I am telling you this now, before it happens, so you will believe it when it happens and you will have faith in me.

How do we show Jesus we love him?

What is Jesus' gift to us?

Sixth Sunday of Easter   Year C   John 14:23-29

The World Does Not Know You

Leader: Today's gospel shares Jesus' prayer for his disciples that they might be one in the Father and in him.

Jesus: I pray for my disciples and everyone who will believe in me because of what they say.

First Disciple: I believe in you, Lord. Will you pray for me?

Jesus: I pray that we all will be together and everyone will believe that you sent me, Father. I have given them the same glory that you gave me so that they will be one as we are one, Father. You live in me and I live in you. I want everyone to know that you sent me here and you love them as much as you love me.

Second Disciple: Does the Father really love me so much?

Jesus: The glory that I have is a gift from you, and I want all of my followers to be with me and to know that. You, Father, have loved me before the world began.

Third Disciple: I wish I knew the Father like you do, Jesus.

Jesus: The world does not know you like I do, but my disciples know that you have sent me here. I have told them about you and I will continue to tell them about you so that your love will be in them and I will be in them.

Fourth Disciple: Teach us more about the Father, Jesus.

How do we get to know God better?

How do we know that God loves us?

Seventh Sunday of Easter   Year C   John 17:20-26

Celebrating the Blessed Trinity

Leader: Jesus is leaving the world. He tells his disciples that when he returns to heaven, the Holy Spirit will come and lead all people to truth.

Narrator: Jesus said to his disciples,

Jesus: I have more to tell you, but it is more than you can understand now.

First Disciple: You have told us so much, Lord.

Jesus: The Spirit will come and take you to the complete truth.

Second Disciple: What is the truth the Spirit will tell us?

Jesus: The Spirit will tell you what he has heard from me and will tell you about things that have not happened yet. The Spirit brings glory to me by telling you my message.

Third Disciple: Will we really be given the complete truth?

Jesus: Everything that is the Father's also belongs to me. That is why I have told you the Spirit will take my message and give it to you.

What does Jesus say is the task of the Holy Spirit?

How does the Holy Spirit bring glory to God the Son?

Sunday After Pentecost   Year C   John 16:12-15

141

Wedding at Cana

Leader: You are probably familiar with Jesus' changing of the water to wine at the wedding of Cana. This first recorded miracle of Jesus is the focus of today's gospel.

Narrator: There was a wedding at Cana in Galilee. Mary, Jesus, and his disciples were there when they ran out of wine. Jesus' mother said to him,

Mary: Jesus, they have no more wine. The groom will be embarrassed.

Jesus: Mother, please don't ask me to help. It is not my time yet.

Narrator: Mary took the waiter aside and said,

Mary: Do what my son tells you to do.

Narrator: Then Jesus addressed the waiters.

Jesus: Fill those six big stone jars with water.

Narrator: The jars held about twenty or thirty gallons and were used by the people for washing. The waiters filled them as Jesus said.

Jesus: Now, draw some water from the jar and take it to the waiter in charge.

Narrator: When the head waiter took a drink, he was amazed. He called the bridegroom over and told him,

Waiter: This is excellent wine! Usually, people serve the best wine first. Then, after everyone has been drinking a while, they serve a lesser wine. You have saved the best wine for last.

Narrator: This first miracle happened in the village of Cana in Galilee. Jesus showed his glory and his disciples believed in him. Jesus, his disciples, and his family then traveled to Capernaum and stayed there for a few days.

What did Jesus mean, "It is not my time yet"?

Why do you think Jesus ended up doing this miracle anyway?

Second Sunday in Ordinary Time   Year C   John 2:1-12

Teaching in the Synagogue

Leader: Today's gospel is from the beginning of Luke's account. In it, Luke explains what he tried to do: carefully trace exactly what happened in the life of Jesus and record it so that we would know that it's true.

Narrator: The story picks up in Nazareth in Galilee where Jesus had been raised. Jesus returned to Galilee, with the power of the Holy Spirit. A citizen from Nazareth spotted a relative who lived in the rural outskirts.

City Bystander: Have you heard about Jesus of Galilee? His teaching is of God.

Country Visitor: Yes, even in the country Jesus has a strong reputation.

Narrator: Jesus entered the synagogue in Nazareth on the Sabbath, as he always did. He took a scroll that had been handed to him, unrolled it, and stood up to read sacred scripture.

Jesus: From the book of the prophet Isaiah: The spirit of the Lord is with me; he has chosen me to tell the good news to the poor. I have been sent by the Lord to tell prisoners about freedom, to help the blind to see and to help all those who suffer. I say, this is the year that the Lord has chosen.

Narrator: Jesus rolled the scroll and handed it back to the assistant. With everyone in the synagogue staring at him, he said,

Jesus: What I have just read has come true through me today.

What do you think it was like for Jesus to come to his hometown?

What did Jesus mean, "What I have just read has come true through me today"?

Third Sunday in Ordinary Time   Year C   Luke 1:1-4, 4:14-21

Doctor, Heal Yourself

Leader: Recall that Jesus went to the synagogue in his own hometown and read from the scriptures. He then told those who gathered that what he read—"the Spirit of the Lord has been given to me"—applied to him. Jesus continued his synagogue teaching.

Jesus: What I have just read in the scriptures has come true.

Narrator: The people began to talk to each other.

First Person: I have heard about Jesus. He teaches about the scriptures so that we can really understand them.

Second Person: I've heard he can cure the sick and make the blind see again.

Third Person: But isn't he Joseph's son, from Galilee?

Fourth Person: Yes, so?

Fifth Person: Some are saying that he is the Messiah, the one we've been waiting for.

Sixth Person: No, that can't be. We have known his family for a long time. How could he be the Messiah?

Jesus: You probably will say to me, "Doctor, heal yourself" and want me to do in this town what I have done in other places. But prophets are not usually recognized in their own hometown. During Elijah's time, there was no rain for over three years and people were starving because of the bad crops. But Elijah was sent to a widow in a distant place. And in Elisha's time there were many lepers, but only a foreign one was healed.

Seventh Person: Listen to him! He is saying that Elijah and Elisha didn't help their people.

Eighth Person: Throw him out of town! He should never be let back here again!

Ninth Person: Throw him off the cliff! Then we know he'll never be back!

Narrator: Jesus slipped through the angry crowd and walked away.

Why do people who know you sometimes not believe you can do something well?

What did Jesus mean by "Doctor, heal yourself"?

Fourth Sunday in Ordinary Time   Year C   Luke 4:21-30

Fishers of People

Leader: Today's gospel tells how—after hearing Jesus' preaching—Simon Peter, James, and John left everything to follow him.

Narrator: Jesus was teaching near the shore of a lake. People were crowding in to hear. Jesus saw some fishermen in two boats close to the bank. Jesus climbed into the boat of Simon Peter and told him,

Jesus: Please take me out on the lake a little, so the people can hear me.

Narrator: Simon Peter rowed Jesus out on the lake and Jesus continued to teach the people. When he was done teaching, he said,

Jesus: Take this boat out into deep water and let your nets down to catch some fish.

Simon Peter: Master, we have been working hard all night trying to catch some fish, but we haven't caught anything. But if you tell me to do it, I will let the nets down again.

Narrator: After he let the nets down, Simon Peter said,

Simon Peter: Look at what's happening! There are so many fish my nets can't hold all of them! John and James! Come here! I need your help!

John: I'm not sure two boats are enough. I've never seen so many fish! The nets are about to break. It's a good thing we have two boats to hold them all.

James: I'm afraid the boats will sink because there are so many fish! And we just came in because we couldn't catch anything!

Narrator: When Simon Peter realized what had happened he fell at the knees of Jesus.

Simon Peter: Lord, don't come near me. I am a sinner.

Jesus: Don't be afraid. From now on, it is people you will catch.

James: I have never seen anything like this. I am going with Jesus.

John: Me too. I want to be with him.

Simon Peter: We will all follow Jesus.

How would you feel if Jesus asked you to fish again after you hadn't caught a fish all night?

What did Jesus mean, "It is people you will catch"?

Fifth Sunday in Ordinary Time   Year C   Luke 5:1-11

Sermon on the Plain

Leader: God blesses those who depend on him for everything. This gospel reminds us to live for the world to come, not for the riches we can gain in this world.

Narrator: Jesus came down a mountain to a level area where his disciples were gathered. There was a large crowd of people from Judea, Jerusalem, and the coast of Tyre and Sidon. Jesus told the people about the meaning of real happiness. He said,

Voice of Poor Person: I am poor. God will bless me and give me his kingdom.

Voice of Hungry Person: I am hungry. God will give me plenty to eat.

Voice of Sad Person: I cry from sadness. God will bless me and I will be happy and laugh.

Voice of a Believer: God will bless me when other people hate me. God will bless me when they insult me and say mean things about me because I believe in the Son of Man. Then I will be happy because I will have my reward in heaven. They treated the prophets the same way.

Voice of a Rich Person: I will be sad, because I am already rich in this life.

Voice of a Satisfied Person: I am filled with earthly riches now. I will be sad later.

Voice of a Happy Person: I laugh now, later I will cry. I will cry because everyone says good things about me now. That is what happened when our own people said good things about the false prophets.

Jesus reverses the usual meaning of happiness. How so?

How do you depend on God?

Sixth Sunday in Ordinary Time   Year C   Luke 6:17, 20-26

Love Your Enemies

Leader: As Jesus concludes his Sermon on the Plain from Luke's gospel, he tells his disciples to be compassionate as the heavenly Father is compassionate.

Jesus: Listen to what I say. Love your enemies and do good to those who hate you.

First Person: I ask God to bless those who curse me, and I pray for those who are mean to me. If someone slaps me on one cheek, I won't stop him from slapping my other.

Second Person: As for me, if someone needs my coat, I will give him my shirt, too. Anything I give I won't expect it to be returned.

Third Person: I will treat others just as I would have them treat me. If I only love those who love me, what good is there in that? Even sinners love people who love them.

Fourth Person: Right, and if I only lend to people who will repay me, what goodness is there in that? Even sinners lend to people who will pay them back.

Jesus: Love your enemies and be good to them. Lend without expecting to be repaid. Then you will receive a great reward. You will be true children of God, for God is good even to those who are unthankful and cruel.

Fifth Person: I will not judge other people, and God won't judge me.

Sixth Person: And I will forgive others and God will forgive me.

Jesus: Whatever you give to others, you will be given in return. You will be given a full measure, packed down, shaken together and spilling over into your lap. For what you give to others is what will be given back to you.

How do you like to be treated?

What do you find hard about Jesus' teaching?

Seventh Sunday in Ordinary Time   Year C   Luke 6:27-38

A Good Tree Will Have Good Fruit

Leader: In today's gospel, Jesus tells a parable with several messages. Among the most important of these is that a person should always speak from what is in his or her heart.

Jesus: Let me tell you a parable about two blind people. They said to each other,

First Blind Person: Come with me. I will lead you where you want to go.

Second Blind Person: How will you know where to walk? You are blind too.

First Blind Person: Take my hand. Trust me.

Jesus: Unfortunately, both were confused. They bumped into each other and fell into a ditch. As for another example, let me tell you about a student speaking with a teacher.

Student: I am not better than my teacher. I have a lot to learn from my teacher.

Teacher: But when you are finished with your studies, you will be like me.

Jesus: Finally, remember it is important not to judge one another, as this conversation shows:

First Person: You have a speck in your eye. Let me take it out for you.

Second Person: Excuse me, but isn't that a log in your eye? When you get the log out of your own eye, you can take the speck out of mine.

Jesus: A good tree will have good fruit, and a bad tree will have bad fruit. Figs come from a fig tree, not from a thorn bush. Grapes come from a grape vine, not from a thorn bush. A good person has a good heart and an evil person has an evil heart. What is in your heart shows in what you say and do.

What is one surprising thing you heard in this gospel?

What is one thing you said or did this week that shows what kind of person you are?

Eighth Sunday in Ordinary Time   Year C   Luke 6:39-45

Lord, I Am Not Worthy

Leader: Jesus' good news is for all people. In today's gospel, a Roman soldier shows dramatic faith in Jesus when his own servant falls ill. Jesus says that he has never found great faith like this even among the chosen people of Israel.

Narrator: Jesus traveled to Capernaum. When he arrived he heard about the Roman soldier and his servant. A Jewish elder relayed the message to Jesus.

Jewish Elder: Jesus, a soldier has sent us here. He has a favorite servant who is very sick. He would like you to heal the servant. This soldier has been very good to our people and has even built a synagogue for us.

Jesus: All right, I will go.

Narrator: Jesus and his disciples set out for the centurion's house. While on their way, one of the soldier's friends came to Jesus with a message.

Friend of the Soldier: We have come for our friend, the Roman soldier. He has said, "I am not worthy to receive you in my house. I am not worthy to speak to you myself. I have many men under my command. I give an order and they obey it. I know what it is to have my orders obeyed. All you have to do is order it and my servant will be healed."

Jesus: I have never found this much faith in me in all of the people of Israel. Go back to the house now.

Narrator: The friend went back to the soldier's house.

Friend of the Soldier: We did as you asked.

Soldier: I know! My servant is cured.

How did the soldier show his faith?

Where have you heard words like the soldier's before: "I am not worthy to receive you . . . only say the word and I shall be healed"?

Ninth Sunday in Ordinary Time   Year C   Luke 7:1-10

Raising of a Young Man

Leader: In the gospel today, Jesus brings a young man back to life. News about Jesus, who can cure the sick and raise the dead, is spreading all over the region.

Narrator: Jesus went to a town called Naim accompanied by his disciples and a great crowd.

First Disciple: Jesus, we are almost into the town of Naim.

Second Disciple: Do you think all these people will go there with us?

Narrator: Near the gate of the town, a dead man was being carried out for burial. The cries of the man's mother could be heard above the crowd.

Woman *(crying)*: My son! My son is dead!

Narrator: Jesus felt sorry for the mother of the dead man.

Jesus: Don't cry.

Narrator: Then touching the dead man, Jesus said,

Jesus: Young man, I tell you to get up.

Young Man *(sitting up)*: I was dead but now I am alive again!

First Witness: This Jesus must be a great prophet.

Second Witness: It was God who did this!

Narrator: News about Jesus spread all around the countryside and all over Judea.

Why did Jesus raise this young man back to life?

What did the witnesses think about Jesus after they saw what happened?

Tenth Sunday in Ordinary Time   Year C   Luke 7:11-17

A Woman Washes Jesus' Feet

Leader: Today's gospel tells how a woman's many sins were forgiven because she showed great love.

Narrator: One of the Pharisees, Simon, invited Jesus to his house for a meal. When Jesus arrived a woman sat at his feet, crying, with her tears falling on Jesus' feet.

Woman (*continuing to cry*): Jesus, I am so happy to be with you. Let me wash your feet with my tears and dry your feet with my hair.

Narrator: Then she kissed his feet and put perfumed oil on them. The Pharisee thought to himself,

Simon the Pharisee: If Jesus were really a prophet, he would know that this woman is a sinner. He should not allow her to touch him.

Jesus: Simon, let me ask you a question.

Simon the Pharisee: Certainly, teacher.

Jesus: What if there were two men who owed money to a moneylender. One of them owed five hundred coins and the other one owed fifty coins. Neither one of them could pay what he owed, so the moneylender told both of them they didn't have to pay him. Which of them was the most grateful to the moneylender?

Simon the Pharisee: I suppose the one who owed the most money.

Jesus: That is right. I came into your house and you did not give me any water to wash my feet with. This woman washed my feet with her tears and dried them with her hair. You did not offer me a kiss, but she has kissed my feet since I came. You gave me no oil for my head, but she covered my feet with perfumed oil. She has great love and that is why her sins have been forgiven her. Those whose love is small will have little forgiven. Woman, your sins are forgiven.

Narrator: Those who were at the table began to talk among themselves.

Guest: Who does he think he is? Does he think he can forgive sins?

Narrator: Then to the woman, Jesus said,

Jesus: Your faith has saved you. Go in peace.

What did Jesus mean by the story of the moneylender?

What is one way you can show great love?

Eleventh Sunday in Ordinary Time   Year C   Luke 7:36-50

You Are the Messiah

Leader: In today's gospel Jesus makes his mission clear. As God's Chosen One, he is destined to suffer much.

Narrator: One day Jesus was praying alone in the presence of his disciples. He put this question to them:

Jesus: Who do the crowds say I am?

First Disciple: Some say you are John the Baptist.

Second Disciple: Some say you are the prophet Elijah.

Third Disciple: Some people say you are one of the prophets of old and that you have come back from the dead.

Jesus: But what about you? Who do you say that I am?

Narrator: It was Peter who spoke up.

Peter: You are the Messiah of God.

Jesus: You must not say that to anyone. None of you! The Son of Man will suffer, be rejected, be put to death, and then be raised up on the third day. Whoever wants to follow me must give up everything. You must take up your cross each day and do as I have done. If you want to save your life you will lose it. But if you give up your life for me, you will save it.

What do you believe about Jesus?

What does it mean to you to have to give up everything for God?

Twelfth Sunday in Ordinary Time   Year C   Luke 9:18-24

The Son of Man Has Nowhere to Rest

Leader: Jesus resolves to face his destiny, to go to Jerusalem where he knows he will be put to death.

Narrator: As he set out for Jerusalem, Jesus sent his messengers ahead of him.

Jesus: It is time for me to go to Jerusalem. Go ahead and get things ready.

Messengers: The Samaritans will not let you pass through their region because you are going to Jerusalem.

First Disciple: You should not let them get away with telling you that you cannot come.

Second Disciple: We can call down fire from heaven to burn their towns.

Jesus: No! We will not destroy any Samaritan villages. We will go another way.

First Person: I will follow you wherever you go.

Jesus: The foxes have their homes, the birds have their nests, but the Son of Man has nowhere to rest.

Second Person: I will follow you, but I must bury my father first.

Jesus: Let the dead bury the dead. Come with me and proclaim the kingdom of God.

Third Person: I will follow you, but first let me take care of things at home.

Jesus: You cannot look back. Once you start to plow, you cannot look back. You will be worthless to the kingdom of God.

What does it mean to follow Jesus wherever he goes?

How can you proclaim the kingdom of God?

Thirteenth Sunday in Ordinary Time   Year C   Luke 9:51-62

The Sending Out of the Disciples

Leader: In today's gospel Jesus sends his disciples out into the world, telling them that they will be like sheep among wolves.

Narrator: Jesus appointed seventy-two disciples beyond the twelve apostles, and sent them out in pairs.

Jesus: I am sending you out ahead of me. You will go in pairs to the same places where I go. The harvest is rich but the workers are few. Ask the harvest master to send more laborers. Go now and remember you will be like lambs surrounded by wolves. Take only what you need. Don't carry a money bag or sandals. Don't speak to people along the way. When you enter a household, say first,

First Disciple: Peace to this household.

Jesus: And if a person of peace lives there, the person will say,

Peaceful Person: Your peace has blessed me. Please stay with us and eat and drink.

Jesus: If there is not a peaceful person living there, your blessing will return to you. If a city welcomes you, eat what they offer you and cure their sick. Then, tell them,

Second Disciple: The kingdom of God will soon be here.

Jesus: If the people of a town do not welcome you say,

Third Disciple: We won't be back! We warn you that the kingdom of God is coming.

Jesus: You can be sure the city of Sodom will be judged easier than that town.

Narrator: Later, the seventy-two came back, rejoicing. Together they told Jesus,

All: Jesus, even Satan obeyed us when we spoke to those possessed in your name!

Jesus: I have seen Satan fall out of the sky, like lightning. This is what I have done; I have given you power over snakes and scorpions and all the power of the enemies. Nothing can hurt you. But what should really make you happy is that your names are written in heaven, not that demons obey you.

Who are the laborers? Who is the harvest master?

What did Jesus say should make the disciples happy?

Fourteenth Sunday in Ordinary Time   Year C   Luke 10:1-12, 17-20

The Good Samaritan

Leader: Today's gospel helps us answer the question "Who is my neighbor?"

Narrator: A lawyer questioned Jesus, trying to ruffle him.

Lawyer: Teacher, what do I have to do to have eternal life?

Jesus: What do the scriptures tell you?

Lawyer: "You shall love the Lord your God with all your heart, with all your soul, with all your strength, and with all your mind; and love your neighbor as yourself."

Jesus: You are right. Do this and you shall have everlasting life.

Lawyer: But who is my neighbor?

Jesus: I will tell you this story. A man is walking from Jerusalem to Jericho. Robbers beat up the man and took his money. They left him sprawled on the ground. A priest walked by and saw him. The priest said to himself,

Priest: I would like to help that man, but I have some very important things to do today. Surely someone else will help him.

Jesus: Next, a Levite of the Jewish priestly class passed by.

Levite: Someone else who has more time than I do will have to help him.

Jesus: Then a man from a Samaria approached. Remember, Samaritans are not friends of the Jews. The Samaritan saw the injured man and said to him,

Samaritan: You have been very badly hurt. I have some water and oil to clean your wounds. I'll take you into town and take care of you until you are better.

Jesus: The Samaritan took the injured man to the local inn. He told the innkeeper,

Samaritan: Here is some money for him to stay here until he is better. Take care of him and if it costs any more than this, I will pay you on my way back through town.

Jesus: Which of these three men, the priest, the Levite, or the Samaritan, was the neighbor to the man who was robbed?

Lawyer: The man who was kind to him and took care of him.

Jesus: Then go and do the same.

Who is your neighbor?

How can you act like the Samaritan?

Fifteenth Sunday in Ordinary Time   Year C   Luke 10:25-37

Martha and Mary

Leader: In today's gospel, Jesus speaks with his friends, Martha and Mary.

Narrator: Jesus came to the village where Martha and Mary lived. Martha welcomed Jesus to her home.

Martha: Jesus, come in! We are so glad to have you in our home. Let me fix you something to eat and drink.

Mary: Jesus, please sit down. I have wanted to talk to you for such a long time.

Narrator: Mary sat on the floor at the feet of Jesus. Meanwhile, Martha was in and out of the room, trying to keep up with the cooking, the setting of the table, and all the different parts of hospitality.

Martha: Lord, I am working so hard to make your visit nice. My sister is just sitting here listening to you. Tell her to help me.

Jesus: Martha, Martha. You are worried about so many things, but there is only one thing that is necessary. This is what Mary has chosen to do, and I will not take this choice away from her.

What is the main message of this gospel?

What can you do to listen to the message of Jesus?

Sixteenth Sunday in Ordinary Time   Year C   Luke 10:38-42

Teach Us to Pray

Leader: In today's gospel, Jesus teaches us how to pray: Our Father who art in heaven. He also reminds us that when we ask in prayer it shall be given to us by our loving Father.

Narrator: When Jesus was finished praying, one of his disciples had a request.

First Disciple: Lord, teach us to pray.

Jesus: Say this when you pray: Our Father, who art in heaven, hallowed be thy name. Thy kingdom come, thy will be done, on earth as it is in heaven. Give us this day our daily bread. And forgive us our trespasses, as we forgive those who trespass against us. Lead us not into temptation, but deliver us from evil.

Narrator: Then Jesus went on to say,

Jesus: Let me tell you a story. It goes like this: A person goes knocking on his friend's door in the middle of the night.

First Person (knocking on the door): Wake up. I need to borrow some bread, because I have a guest and I don't have any food to share.

Second Person: Leave me alone. We are all in bed for the night. Come back tomorrow.

First Person (continuing to knock): Please let me borrow some bread for my guest. I will keep on asking for your help until you give it to me.

Second Person: All right, all right. I suppose the only way to get some sleep is to give you what you need.

Jesus: Ask for something and you will receive it. If you look, you will find. If you knock, the door will be opened. Anyone who asks will receive. Anyone who looks will find. The door will be opened for anyone who knocks. There is not a father who would give his son a snake if he asked for a fish. No father would give his son a scorpion if he asked for an egg. Even you, with all your sins, know how to be good fathers to your children. You must know that the Father is even more willing to give the Holy Spirit to anyone who asks.

Why do we call God "our Father"?

What is the meaning of the story that Jesus told about the person who knocked on his friend's door in the middle of the night?

Seventeenth Sunday in Ordinary Time   Year C   Luke 11:1-13

Parable of the Rich Fool

Leader: Jesus tells us that material possessions do not make our lives secure, even when we have more than we need.

Narrator: A person in the crowd said to Jesus,

Person: Jesus, tell my brother to give me my share of what our father left us when he died.

Jesus: Why are you asking me to settle your argument? Everyone listen. You should not be greedy. A person may own a lot of things, but that will not give him a carefree life. Let me tell you a story about a very rich man. The rich man thought to himself,

Rich Man: This was a very good year. My farm produced such a big crop, I don't even have a place large enough to store it all. I will have to tear down my barns and build bigger barns. Then I will be able to store all the grain I have grown this year, and all my other things too. Then I can say to myself, "You have stored enough to last for many years. Enjoy yourself! Eat, drink, and relax."

Jesus: But God will say to him, "You fool! Tonight you will die. Then will it matter if you have a lot stored or a little stored? Who will get all of your things then?" That is what happens to a person who does everything for himself or herself, and nothing for God.

What could the rich man have done with the extra crops he had?

Why don't material possessions guarantee our lives will be secure?

Eighteenth Sunday in Ordinary Time   Year C   Luke 12:13-21

Like a Thief in the Night

Leader: We do not know when Jesus will come again so we must live a life that is pleasing to God. Jesus tells us to always be ready.

Jesus: Do not be afraid, little flock. Your Father wants to give you his kingdom. Sell what you have and give to the poor. Get purses that will never wear out. Your treasure will be safe in heaven, where no one can steal it and moths cannot destroy it. Be ready! Be like this servant who is waiting for the master to return.

Servant: Welcome home, Master! I have stayed awake waiting for you.

Master: I am pleased with you. I will take care of you.

Servant: It did not matter if you came home at midnight or dawn, I was ready for you.

Jesus: You know that no one would let a thief break in if they knew when the thief was coming. So be prepared. The Son of Man will come when you do not expect him.

Narrator: Then Peter asked Jesus,

Peter: Is this parable for just us, or is it for the whole world?

Jesus: Who do you think is the wise and faithful servant? The Master will say,

Master: You have been wise and faithful. I will put you in charge of all that I own.

Jesus: But as for the servant who says,

Servant: I don't think my master is coming home soon. I am going to be lazy. I am going to make everyone else do my work while I do nothing.

Jesus: The Master will say upon returning,

Master: I have come back. I know you did not expect me at this time. I must punish you and throw you out with the other servants who cannot be trusted. You knew what you were supposed to do and you did not do it. If you did not know what you were supposed to do, you would not be punished as harshly.

Jesus: When God gives you many things, he will expect much from you. If you have not been given as much, not as much will be expected from you.

What can you do to prepare for Jesus?

Have you been given a lot or given a little from God?

Nineteenth Sunday in Ordinary Time   Year C   Luke 12:32-48

I Have Come to Set the World on Fire

Leader: Jesus offers strong words in today's gospel. He says that he has come to challenge people not to accept things as they are.

Jesus: I have come to set the world on fire, and how I wish the blaze was already ignited!

First Disciple: Why would Jesus want to set the world on fire?

Second Disciple: I wonder what kind of fire?

Jesus: I have a baptism to receive and pain to endure. Do you think I have come to bring peace to the earth?

Third Disciple: Yes, Lord, I did think you came to bring peace.

Jesus: No, the opposite is true. People will have to choose sides. A family of five will be three against two. Fathers and sons will be against each other as will mothers and daughters and mothers-in-law and daughters-in-law.

What kind of fire did Jesus come to start?

What do you find hard about following Jesus?

Twentieth Sunday in Ordinary Time   Year C   Luke 12:49-53

The Narrow Door

Leader: In today's gospel Jesus says that people from all corners of the earth will come to take their place at the great feast in the kingdom of God.

Narrator: Jesus taught in many towns and villages on the way to Jerusalem. On one of the stops, a bystander asked him,

Bystander: Are there only a few who will be saved?

Jesus: It will be like many trying to get through a narrow door. Many will try to get in, but only a few will be able to. It will be like this:

First Person: The master has locked the door. I have to get in. Please let me in.

Master: I do not know you.

First Person: But I ate and drank with you. You taught in my hometown.

Master: I do not know you. Get away from me, you evil one.

First Person: Please do not throw me out. Abraham, Isaac, Jacob, and all the prophets are safe in God's kingdom. There are many people who come from all directions and are sitting down to feast in God's kingdom.

Jesus: And some who are first now will be last then. And some who are last now in the eyes of the world will be first in the kingdom of God.

Who will enter the kingdom of God?

Who are some people who are "first" now? Who are some people who are "last" now?

Twenty-First Sunday in Ordinary Time   Year C   Luke 13:22-30

Conduct of Invited Guests

Leader: Jesus tells us to be kind to those who have less than we do. We should be kind to them without expecting anything in return. But remember, our God in heaven sees everything.

Narrator: On the Sabbath, Jesus went for a meal at the house of one of the leading Pharisees.

Jesus: I am going to tell you a parable about guests who came to a wedding feast. Their conversation went like this:

First Guest: I am going to sit myself at the main table. That is where the most important people are sitting.

Second Guest: Well, I should have a better seat than you because I am more important than you are.

Jesus: When you are invited to a dinner, you should not say this:

First Guest: I am going to sit in this place of honor at the table.

Jesus: If you do, the host may say:

Host: I am sorry but I have to ask you to move to a less important place. That place you are sitting in is saved for someone else.

Jesus: Rather, when you are invited to a dinner, you should say and do this:

Second Guest: I am going to sit in the lowest seat at the most out of the way table.

Jesus: Then, this may happen. The host could say,

Host: My friend, come take a better seat.

Jesus: Then you will receive honor among the other guests. If you put yourself above others, you will be put lower. If you humble yourself, you will be honored. When you give a dinner, do not invite your friends and relatives or wealthy neighbors. They could repay you by inviting you to their house for a meal. When you have a dinner, invite beggars, the crippled, and the blind. They cannot repay you now, but you will be repaid at the resurrection.

When was a time you put the needs of others before your own needs?

Why is it important to be humble?

Twenty-Second Sunday in Ordinary Time   Year C   Luke 14:1, 7-14

Give Away Everything You Own

Leader: In today's gospel, Jesus says that the one who does not freely give up his or her possessions cannot be called a disciple.

Narrator: Great crowds pressed near Jesus and he turned and spoke with them.

Jesus: To be my disciple, you must love me more than you love even your mother or father, your wife and children, and your brothers and sisters. You must love me more than your own life if you want to be my follower. You must carry your own cross and come with me. Think about it this way, what if you were going to build a tower?

First Person: I am going to build a tower. I must sit down and figure out how to do it and how much it will cost.

Second Person: I am going to build a tower too but I'm just going to start building it. I hope I have enough money to pay for it.

Jesus: But later, the second person finds out there isn't enough money to finish the tower.

Third Person: Look at that! An unfinished tower. That person started to build a tower but did not have enough money to finish the job.

Jesus: Or think about a king who is about to go to war against another king.

First King: I have ten thousand soldiers. The other king has twenty thousand soldiers. I don't think I can win this battle. Messengers! Go to the other king and tell him this:

Messenger: I have a message from my king. You have more soldiers than we have. We do not want to fight. We want peace.

Second King: Your offer is accepted.

Jesus: So in the same way, you cannot be my disciples unless you give away everything you own.

What is the message in the stories of the tower and the king preparing for battle?

What is the thing you would find the hardest to give away out of love for Jesus?

Twenty-Third Sunday in Ordinary Time   Year C   Luke 14:25-33

More Joy in Heaven

Leader: Jesus spent time with sinners and told them about God's forgiveness. In heaven there will be joy over one sinner who asks for forgiveness.

Narrator: The tax collectors and sinners all wanted to be near Jesus and hear what he had to say. A Pharisee said,

Pharisee: Look at Jesus. He welcomes sinners and will even eat with them.

Jesus: If you were a farmer with one hundred sheep and lost one of them, what would you do? Wouldn't you leave the other ninety-nine and go to look for the lost sheep? And when you found it, you would be so happy that you would carry the sheep home and tell your neighbors and friends,

Farmer: Be happy with me! I lost one of my sheep and now I have found it!

Jesus: I tell you that there is more happiness in heaven with one sinner who repents than with ninety-nine who do not need to repent. And what about the old woman who loses a coin?

Woman: I know I had ten pieces of silver and now I can only find nine. I am going to search everywhere until I find it. I will sweep the whole house if I have to, but I will find that piece of silver. Oh! Here it is! I found it! Look, I found what I lost! Come and be happy with me.

Jesus: The angels will have the same kind of joy when a sinner repents.

Why did Jesus spend time with sinners?

What do the stories of the lost sheep and lost coin mean?

Twenty-Fourth Sunday in Ordinary Time   Year C   Luke 15:1-10 (shorter)

You Cannot Serve Two Masters

Leader: Today's gospel reminds us that God, not money, should be what is most important to us.

Jesus: There was a rich man who had a steward who was being dishonest with his money. The rich man said to the steward,

Rich Man: I have heard you have been dishonest with my money. I am going to fire you unless you give me a reason not to.

Steward: What am I going to do? He is going to fire me! I don't want to dig ditches and I don't want to beg for money. I know what I'll do! I'll talk to everyone who owes my master money. I will reduce their debt. *(to first debtor)* What do you owe my master?

First Debtor: I owe one hundred jars of oil.

Steward: Take your invoice and make it fifty jars. I'll change my invoice too.

First Debtor: Oh, thank you! Now I owe you a favor!

Steward *(to second debtor)***:** What do you owe my master?

Second Debtor: One hundred measures of wheat.

Steward: Quick! Take your invoice and make it eighty measures of wheat.

Jesus: The rich man heard what the steward did.

Rich Man: I heard what you did. Even though you were dishonest with me and my debtors, I must give you credit. You found a way to have people owe you favors. You were very smart, just like me.

Jesus: Remember, dishonest people are comfortable with their own kind. Use what you have in this world to make friends, but make sure that what you do on earth will not change your welcome in heaven. If you can be trusted in little things, you can be trusted in bigger things. If you are not to be trusted in little things, you cannot be trusted in bigger things. If you cannot be trusted with the wealth of this world, you cannot be trusted with everlasting riches in heaven. If you cannot be trusted with someone else's money, you cannot be trusted with your own. A servant cannot serve two masters. He will either hate one and love the other, or pay attention to one and ignore the other. You cannot give yourself to God and money.

Why did the rich man come to admire the steward?

Why can't you give yourself to God and money?

Twenty-Fifth Sunday in Ordinary Time   Year C   Luke 16:1-13

Rich Man and Poor Lazarus

Leader: Today's gospel reminds us that how we treat others in this world affects our standing in the next world.

Narrator: Jesus told the following story about a rich man and a poor man named Lazarus. The rich man said,

Rich Man: Lazarus, you lay every day at the gates to my house. You let my dogs lick the sores on your legs and arms.

Lazarus: Please sir, I am so hungry. Just give me the scraps from your table. Even that would be more than I have now.

Jesus: But the rich man never helped Lazarus. Lazarus died and was carried by angels to heaven, where he stayed by Abraham. The rich man also died, and was sent to a place of fire. In his pain the rich man saw Abraham a long way off with Lazarus.

Rich Man: Please Father Abraham. Have pity on me. Send Lazarus with some water for me. I am so hot and thirsty in this fire.

Abraham: My child, remember that you were well off during your life, and Lazarus was in agony. Now, he has found comfort here and you have found pain. But no one can cross from your side to this side and no one can cross from this side to your side.

Rich Man: Then I ask that you send Lazarus to my father's house. I have five brothers that need to be warned to repent so they do not come to this place of fire.

Abraham: Moses and the prophets have warned them. They should listen.

Rich Man: If someone would come from the dead to warn them, then they would listen.

Abraham: If they will not listen to Moses and the prophets, then they will not be convinced even if someone should rise from the dead to warn them.

What could the rich man have done to help Lazarus?

Who rose from the dead to tell us about heaven and warn us about hell?

Twenty-Sixth Sunday in Ordinary Time   Year C   Luke 16:19-31

Increase Our Faith

Leader: Along with the disciples of today's gospel, we beg the Lord to "increase our faith!"

Narrator: The apostles said to Jesus,

Apostle: Increase our faith!

Jesus: If you had faith the size of a mustard seed, you could say to that sycamore tree,

Faithful Person: Move from here and plant yourself in the sea.

Jesus: And it would obey you. If you had a servant who was working in the fields would you say to him, come and eat with me at my table? No, you would say,

Master: Fix my supper. Put on your apron and wait on me while I eat and drink. You can eat and drink later.

Jesus: Would you be grateful to the servant who was only carrying out his orders? It is much the same with you who hear me. When you have done all that you have been commanded to do, say

Faithful Person: We are useless servants. We have only done our duty.

What would you do if you had faith the size of a mustard seed?

What is your duty to God?

Twenty-Seventh Sunday in Ordinary Time   Year C   Luke 17:5-10

Healing of Ten Lepers

Leader: In today's gospel, after Jesus heals ten lepers, only one, a Samaritan who was a foreigner, came back to thank Jesus.

Narrator: Jesus was traveling to Jerusalem. He passed by the borders of Samaria and Galilee. He was entering a small village when ten lepers met him. (Lepers are people with leprosy, a disease that causes large skin sores.) The lepers began to call out to Jesus,

First Leper: Jesus, Master, have pity on us!

Jesus: Go and show yourselves to the priests.

Narrator: On their walk to the priests, this is what happened:

Second Leper: Look! My sores are going away!

Third Leper: I feel so much better!

Fourth Leper: We are all cured!

Samaritan Leper: I am going back to Jesus to thank him for curing me.

Narrator: The Samaritan leper left the others and found Jesus. He fell on his knees in front of Jesus.

Samaritan Leper: Jesus, thank you! You have cured me! I will always be grateful to you. You have done what no one else could do.

Jesus: But all ten of you were cured. Where are the other nine? You are a Samaritan and you were the only one to come back and give thanks. Stand up and go home now. Your faith has saved you.

What is surprising about the story?

When do you say "thank you" to Jesus?

Twenty-Eighth Sunday in Ordinary Time   Year C   Luke 17:11-19

Pray Always

Leader: Jesus reminds us about the need to pray always and to never lose heart because God always hears our prayers.

Narrator: Jesus addressed this parable to his disciples:

Jesus: Once there was a judge in a certain town. The judge did not respect God or people. He did not do what was right. A widow was being mistreated and she kept coming to the judge, saying,

Widow: I am a poor widow. Do what is right, and make my enemies do what is right. I am going to keep coming to you every day until I am treated fairly and my enemies are punished.

Jesus: The judge thought to himself,

Judge: I don't care anything about this woman. But I am getting tired of her coming to me all the time. I will give her what she wants so she will leave me alone.

Jesus: God is like that. If you call out to him night and day, he will give justice to you. Do you think he will make you wait? No, he will give you swift justice. But when the Son of Man comes, will he find any faith on the earth?

Why did the judge give the woman what she wanted?

What is Jesus' lesson about prayer in this parable?

Twenty-Ninth Sunday in Ordinary Time   Year C   Luke 18:1-8

Be Merciful to Me, a Sinner

Leader: In the gospel today, Jesus compares a Pharisee and a tax collector. Remember in Jesus' time, Pharisees were considered to be holy people and tax collectors were considered to be sinners.

Narrator: Jesus told this parable to people who thought they were holier and better than other people.

Jesus: A Pharisee and a tax collector went to the temple to pray. First the Pharisee prayed proudly with his head upright.

Pharisee: Thank you God for not making me like other people, sinful and greedy like this tax collector. I fast twice a week and I give the right amount of money to the Temple.

Jesus: Then the tax collector, with head bowed, prayed humbly.

Tax Collector: Have mercy on me Lord, I am a sinner.

Jesus: What the tax collector did pleased God. But the Pharisee did not please God for everyone who exalts himself or herself will be humbled and everyone who humbles himself or herself will be exalted.

The Pharisee thought he was doing right. What was he doing wrong?

The tax collector thought he was doing wrong. What was he doing right?

Thirtieth Sunday in Ordinary Time   Year C   Luke 18:9-14

Staying With Zacchaeus

Leader: Today's gospel reminds us that the reason Jesus came into the world was to seek and find those who have lost their way to God.

Narrator: Jesus and his disciples were in the city of Jericho, the hometown of Zacchaeus, a very rich tax collector. Zacchaeus was anxious to see what kind of man Jesus was, but since he was so short in height he couldn't see over the crowd of people who had lined the way.

Zacchaeus: They said Jesus is coming this way. I won't be able to see him because I'm so short. I know! I'll climb that sycamore tree so I can get a good view of him.

Narrator: When Jesus noticed Zacchaeus in the tree, he stopped and said to him,

Jesus: Zacchaeus, come down. I'm going to stay at your house today.

Zacchaeus (*hurrying down the tree*)**:** Jesus! I am so pleased that you will stay with me. Please, come!

Narrator: Everyone complained when they saw what was happening.

First Person: He is going to a sinner's house!

Second Person: Why would he chose to go with a tax collector, a sinner?

Narrator: Zacchaeus heard what they were saying about him. So he said to Jesus,

Zacchaeus: Lord, I will give half of my property to the poor. If I have cheated anyone, I will pay them back four times what I took from them.

Jesus: Today, salvation has come to this house. Zacchaeus has shown you what it means to be a son of Abraham. The Son of Man has come to find and save what was lost.

How did Zacchaeus show he was sorry for his sins?

Why did Jesus come to earth?

Thirty-First Sunday in Ordinary Time   Year C   Luke 19:1-10

Questions About the Resurrection

Leader: The Sadducees were leaders of the Jewish people who had money and influence. They tried to trick Jesus into saying things against Jewish law.

Narrator: The Sadducees did not believe that people would rise to life after death and they asked Jesus these questions to try to show he was wrong about resurrection.

First Sadducee: Teacher, Moses wrote that if a man dies and leaves a wife but no child, that man's brother should marry the widow.

Second Sadducee: What if there were seven brothers? The first one married and died, and he had no children. Then, the second brother married the widow and he died, without having children. Then the third married, then the fourth and so on. All seven brothers died without having had any children.

Third Sadducee: Finally the widow herself died. At the resurrection, whose wife will she be? Remember, all seven brothers married her.

Jesus: The people in this world get married. In the world which is to come, no one who is worthy to rise from the dead will either marry or die again. They will be like the angels and will not die, because they are children of God. Moses showed that people will live again in the story of the burning bush. Moses called God the God of Abraham and of Isaac and of Jacob. God is not the God of the dead but of the living. All people are in fact alive.

Why were the Sadducees trying to trick Jesus?

What does it mean to say that God is "God of the living, not of the dead"?

Thirty-Second Sunday in Ordinary Time   Year C   Luke 20:27-38

Nation Will Rise Against Nation

Leader: In today's gospel, Jesus tells us that those who are strong and keep the faith until the end will save their lives.

Narrator: Some of Jesus' disciples were admiring the architecture and stonework of the Temple.

First Disciple: The Temple is so beautiful.

Second Disciple: Look at the beautiful stones and all the candles and gifts people have given.

Jesus: The day will come when the Temple is torn down and not one stone will be left on another.

Third Disciple: When will this happen, Teacher?

Fourth Disciple: What will be the sign that this will happen?

Jesus: People will come and claim to be me. Don't be fooled by them. They will say the time has come. Do not follow them. You must not be afraid when you hear about wars and uprisings. These things will happen first, but the end will not come right away after that. Nation will rise against nation and kingdom against kingdom. There will be great earthquakes, diseases, and hunger. You will see frightening signs in the sky. But even before this happens, you will be mistreated and arrested. They will bring you to synagogues and prisons and put you on trial before kings and governors. This will all be done because of your faith in me. This will be your time to witness to your faith. Do not worry before about what you will say. I will give you words and wisdom that your enemies cannot disagree with. You will be betrayed by your parents, brothers, relatives, and friends, and some of you will be put to death. All will hate you because of me, yet not a hair on your head will be harmed. You will be saved by your faithfulness.

What time is Jesus describing?

How can you be saved from all of the evil of the world?

Thirty-Third Sunday in Ordinary Time   Year C   Luke 21:5-19

Jesus Christ, the King

Leader: Jesus Christ is king, even as he hangs on the cross.

Narrator: As Jesus hung on the cross, the leaders and the people made fun of him.

Bystander: He saved others, let him save himself if he is the Messiah of God, the Chosen One.

Narrator: Next some soldiers taunted him.

First Soldier: Are you thirsty, Jesus? Have some of this sour wine.

Second Soldier: If you are the king of the Jews, save yourself.

Third Soldier: I'm putting a sign on the cross that says, "This is the King of the Jews."

Narrator: Even one of the criminals hanging on a cross beside Jesus abused him.

First Criminal: Aren't you the Messiah? If you are, save yourself and us.

Narrator: But a criminal on the other side of Jesus told him to stop.

Second Criminal: Don't you fear God? We have the same punishment that he has, but we deserve it. We are paying for what we have done. But Jesus has done nothing wrong. Jesus, remember me when you enter your reign.

Jesus: I assure you: this day you will be with me in paradise.

Why didn't Jesus save himself from dying on the cross?

How do you imagine it will be like to meet Jesus in paradise?

Last Sunday in Ordinary Time   Year C   Luke 23:35-43